D o n

praying:
what is your It?

MATTHEW 7:7
Praying with Purpose & Focus

DEDICATION

I want to dedicate this book to my best friend, my wife, Trish. Through the years, she has never failed to pray for me and to encourage me. Her faith spurred me on when faith was not my strength. During the years preceding this book, she listened as I shared what God was saying to me. She followed me unquestionably around the world always giving up much each time, yet never letting it show. She became my sounding board on many a long road trip and during many a late evening. She was patient as the book was being written, and I learned much from her as the Holy Spirit spoke through her. God has used her more than anyone else in my life to shape and mold me. I am very thankful to have her in my life.

THANKS

To my family who have allowed me to share their its and who have shared mine. They have consistently, persistently and fervently prayed for me. Through the years not all of our its have been discussed or shared, but they seemed to always know what was the it they needed to pray for in my life and in each other's. I love them deeply and owe much to them. Much of what is in this book has been lived out with them. They have allowed God to work in the midst of their its and, at times humbling themselves before Him and allowing Him to change their its to His. May they always have a heart that wants His its more than their own.

I give thanks to my Lord who has expressed His <u>it</u> to me many times, even when I was resistant to wanting what He wanted. He has never failed to intercede for me, and He still does. May He always find me to be submissive to His it even when I do not understand. May He find me to be a child of His whose submissiveness is not conditioned upon my understanding of what He desires.

TABLE of CONTENTS

Title Page	1
Dedication	3
Thanks	3
1 Introduction	7
2 Ask and **it** …	11
3 Examples of **It** Prayers in Scripture	17
4 God's **It**	26
5 Shepherding God's People to Pray for **It**	34
6 Petitioning for **It**	45
7 Interceding for **It**	50
8 Confessing **It**	55
9 Giving Thanks for **It**	59
10 Lamenting for **It**	63
11 The **Its** of the Early Church and Paul	67
12 Conclusion	69

© 2013 Don Pierson
All Scriptures listed are from the King James Version of the Bible.

INTRODUCTION

I was driving thru San Ignacio, Belize when a very frantic woman flagged me down and jumped in my car. I could hardly understand her, but it was obvious she was filled with fear. A sense of urgency had grasped her. She immediately started screaming, "Drive! Hurry my little boy has swallowed a marble!" She continued yelling instructions about where to turn. I was driving as fast as I could, but my heart was going faster than my car. The whole time I am praying to myself, at least I thought I was praying to myself. I looked and saw her face and realized I was screaming my prayer. She had become totally silent and was just staring at me as I was praying. I am sure at first she thought I was some kind of nut, but then the two of us exploded forth with the same prayer, "Lord, help! We don't know what to do but you do, remove this marble!"

I thought we would never get to her home. This woman had tried to help the boy, but when she realized she could not, she left him in the arms of her young daughter and ran for help. I was the first person she found that would even pay attention to her. As we rushed out of the car and up the steps, her daughter threw open the door, and standing behind her was the little boy choking. I was still praying as I entered the room, but before I could take a couple of steps inside, the marble came flying out in a flood of vomit. Let me tell you something, that was the most beautiful vomit I have ever seen. The woman grabbed her son and then grabbed me. She started to unleash all the joy in her heart. As I drove away, I remember weeping and saying, "Thank you Lord!" over and over again. This lady had an **it,** and she gave her **it** to me.

Willie was a young 13 year old kid when I found him sleeping in the corner of the house we were building in Belize. That young boy captured my heart from the first time I saw him. He wasn't a saint by any means. In fact, he was constantly causing me extra heartache, but I could not seem to walk away from him. One time I was walking down the street when a young man walked up to me and asked if I wanted to buy a camera. He held out a camera that looked very familiar to me. I turned it over and immediately knew it was mine. I said, "This is mine! Where did you get it?" He said, "From Willie!" I had to buy back my own camera. Another time Willie was working with me, and I noticed he had a brand new machete. Willie didn't own anything and everything he had came from me or a couple of other men in the church. I could tell by his look though that something wasn't right. I said, "Willie, tell me where you got this machete." After much questioning, he told me he had taken it from the store next to the church. He took me to the church and showed me how he had been climbing on the roof and jumping on to the roof of the store. He would then lift up the tin, drop into the store, take what he wanted and climb back out. He showed me how he had been hiding everything in the attic of the church by lifting up its tin and laying his stuff inside. Needless to say, I was a little upset. We collected all of his stuff, went next door, gave it all back, and told them they might want to fix their roof. The shop keeper was a friend. He laughed and then scolded Willie. Willie caused me a lot of grief, but he also brought me a lot of joy. Willie stayed with me nearly every day all day long for several years. Then one day I caught him in a horrific sin. I was mad. He was furious and ashamed. He made up his mind he would kill me. He tried everything he could to find a weapon. The other young men all came and warned me, but I loved Willie more than I feared Willie. I prayed. Oh, did I pray for that boy. He became my **it**. Before he could do anything to me, he stole a horse that had not been broken. The horse had been running with a few others in the cemetery (that was normal in Belize at that time). Willie tried to ride the horse but it threw him onto a grave stone and broke his back. He was left paralyzed. The church and I prayed for Willie with all that was in us. Once again Willie became our **it**. God did some amazing things during the next year in Willie's life, but he never did walk again. He did turn to the Lord and began working with the youth. God didn't do what we asked, but God answered our prayers. Willie died a few years ago, and to this day, I cannot think of that young boy without tearing up. That boy made me pray, a lot!

Through the years I have learned to categorize my prayers by the **its** I have had. My first **it** was for my own salvation. My second was for a girl friend, and God gave me my wife. One **it** prayer I remember was when I home watching my little girl. She was just a newborn at the time. I was at home alone with her when God began to ask me, "What kind of daddy are you going to be?" I wept so hard when I offered Him this **it**, "Lord, I want to be the best daddy I can be, but I don't know how. Help me to be the best daddy I can be!" That night our church was in revival. God began to call me to preach, but I had such a hard time talking to people. I was so afraid of people. But the calling of God was so strong I rushed to the altar and prayed another **it** that day, "Lord, open my mouth!" He took away the fear of people and filled my heart with boldness. I have never shut my mouth since. You may ask, "How are these two **its** related?" Well, that's easy. In order for me to be the best daddy I could be, I needed to not be afraid.

Through the years, God's people have granted me the sacred trust of sharing their **it** prayers. In those moments, their **its** became my **its**, and I joined them in anticipating God moving in their lives. The salvation of many a lost man weighed heavy on my heart as their loved ones would say, pray for them. Men like Buddy, Buck, Jake, Moses, and Jack became my **it** during those seasons of sowing, watering, and eventually, harvesting. Praying for them became my heart cry and not just another name on a list. I rejoiced as I watched God answer my **it** prayers for them.

Sometime and somewhere I noticed my prayers for my family became **it** prayers too. In my journals there seems to be reoccurring prayers for various ones. These were prayers that were given birth from the heart and not the head. When these prayers were answered, they were the ones that gave birth to the greatest praise. These **its** have become part of my testimony, my story of God's wonder-working power as He has responded to the likes of me. At some point, my family decided to intentionally make **it** praying a part of our tradition. Each day the **it** prayers of my family are lifted up before the throne of God. Generally around the Christmas holiday my wife begins the process of collecting the **it** prayers, the heart cries of our family. We sometimes express these as the one thing we long for God to do among us in the next year. She puts them all together and sends them to each of us, and they become a natural part of our devotions each day. As a family, we have seen God do some amazing things as He has answered our **it** prayers. These answers have become a part of our testimony.

In working with churches I often ask the pastor and leaders, what is the one thing you long for God to do among you in the next year? Most have never thought in this way, but when offered the challenge, they are usually quick to share a desire that is so dear to them they are unable to share it without tears. **It** prayers are like that. In the pages ahead, I am going to try to share the place that **it** prayers have in Scripture and challenge you to make **it** a major part of your life and that of your church. May the Lord reveal to you what is on His heart, His **it** and may His **it** become your heart desire as well.

2

ASK AND IT... MATTHEW 7:7

While studying the prayers of Scripture, I made, what was to me anyway, an amazing discovery. Where are the prayer lists? There is an obvious absence of prayer lists in the prayers of Scripture! You know those unending lists of prayer requests that fill our church bulletins and pews each Wednesday night. At first I thought I must be mistaken. But the more I studied, the more obvious it became. There are very few, if any, prayer lists found in the prayers of Scripture. In fact, it is very rare that a person is found praying in Scripture for even two things and when you do, it is directly related to the main **it** of the prayer. The point being, whenever another request appears in a prayer it is always connected to the main **it** or desire of the person who is praying. The more I studied, the more obvious it became, that **it** praying is the norm of Scripture. Is **it** praying your norm of praying? Is **it** the norm for your church's prayer meetings?

The second realization was that these individuals were only asking for what they wanted and not something somebody else wanted. When they did pray for someone else's **it,** that became their **it**. They joined their heart with the other person's need. In each case they didn't have to be asked twice concerning their **it**. They could declare it clearly without any thought. They knew what they needed or wanted and did not need to have a list to remind them of what their **it** was. When they closed their eyes to pray, their **it** constantly stood before them. When they closed their eyes at night, they dreamed of **it**. Their **it** consumed their thoughts during the day and night. They could not escape their **it**. (I Samuel 1, Luke 18:35-43) Can you escape your **it**? If so, then it is probably because your **it** hasn't grabbed your heart. Not yet anyway.

The third thing I discovered was the amount of emotion connected to the person's **it**. This **it** was their heart cry. This person was consumed by a deep passion, yearning for their **it** to become a reality. They longed for God to hear and to grant their **it**. Their prayers express deep hunger, thirst, anguish, brokenness, desperateness, a deep yearning of the soul. Weeping, tearing of clothes, wailing, mourning, begging, pleading, fasting, crying out are just some of the words God uses to describe the way they prayed for their **it**. They are found praying for hours, throughout the night, for years, for the desire of their heart. These prayers are passionate and fervent because they explode from the person's heart or soul. These are not prayers that are birthed by some kind of mental religious activity; they arise out of hearts longing to be heard. Like those of Isaiah 62:6-7, they know no rest and they give God no rest because they can't help themselves. They aren't trying to be fervent or frequent in their praying, they can't help themselves from being so. (Nehemiah 1; Luke 8:41-56)

Perhaps the most convicting thing has been the realization of how much time they spent praying for their **it**. They would pray and fast for weeks for one thing and seemed to have no problem doing so. An all night of prayer was nothing to them, and they did not need a lot to pray about in order to pray a long time. As long as they had their **it,** that was all that was necessary to cause them to cry out through the night. This is such a contrast to the church of today. Our prayer meetings start and end on time. In fact, most are over before they start. There is very little emotion unless there is a major immediate tragedy. For the church today to pray all night we have to take shifts and there better be a lot to pray for. The idea of today's church praying all night for one thing in agonizing prayer is foreign to us. Yet some of the prayer warriors of old spent years praying for their **it**. Have you ever prayed all night for one thing? Has your church?

As a church planter in North Carolina, during the early years of our church's start, we would gather regularly at homes and pray all night for God's anointing and leadership as we sought to fulfill the Great Commission. My children at the time were very young, and they would join us and eventually fall asleep in a corner somewhere as we cried out to God.

As a missionary in Belize, I remember a time gathering at Armenia Baptist Church for an all night prayer meeting. This church was in a very poor bush community, but these people were not poor in spirit. That night we pierced the darkness not just with the little lantern that hung on a wire in the center of the room, but with our cries as we sought God to move among the community and to save family and friends.

Let me alert you to the fact that the prayers of the saints of Scripture were no vain repetitions but persistent prayers their Heavenly Father welcomed. It was while studying these prayers that I discovered that the difference between a vain repetition and a persistent prayer is the place of origin. A vain repetition begins and ends in the *mind*. A persistent prayer begins and ends in the *heart*. The words have very little to do with whether a prayer is a vain repetition or a persistent prayer. Two prayers can sound exactly alike but that which determines if it is a vain repetition or a persistent prayer is the presence or absence of a heart cry. Prayer should never be a mere mental or religious activity. Drawing near unto God with our mouths has never impressed Him. God has always sought to have our hearts, and if there is a time He should always have it, it would be when we seek His face in prayer.

It should be noted that their faith was seen, not in the fact that they cried out only once for their **it**, but they could not stop asking for their **it**. We often think that to ask more than once is a sign of lack of faith, yet the examples of Scripture give evidence to the exact opposite. These individuals brought their **it** over and over again because they believed God heard them and would answer them. They cried unto Him because they believed He heard them. Some of the most passionate prayers of Scripture are those known as the Prayers of Crying Out. There are over a thousand times where the Scripture records God's people cried out unto Him. These prayers of crying out have at least five dominate factors driving them—

1.) They were not foreign to the individual but were as natural as a child crying out to his/her earthly parent. They were simply crying out to God because He is their father.

2.) They were expressions of the intimate relationship that the person already enjoyed with God or one for which they longed.

3.) They were the result of the belief that God heard them when they cried out and not in order to get Him to hear them. This is the difference between those in the days of Elijah who cried out over and over again to Baal so as to wake him up. These do not seek to wake God up or to wear Him down; they cry out because they need Him and know He is listening.

4.) They came out of the overflow of a heart that needed to be heard. The person who cries out is one who has been humbled. They have no other choice; they could not stop even if others tried to stop them. Just check out the story of Bartimaeus (Mark 10:46-52), and you will find a man who had an **it**, who was desperate for **it**, knew God was near and was filled with hope; thus no one could silence him. This kind of person forgets about what others think and will do things they normally may not do. If you need a present day example take a trip to the Intensive Care Waiting Unit on any given day, and there you will find such individuals.

5.) They originate from a desperate heart, a heart that needs help and needs it now. (Isaiah 62:6-7; Luke 18:1-8)

It doesn't seem to matter whether there is one person praying or the whole people of God—the characteristics are the same. They have an **it**, and they are bringing their **it** to God. The one accord is obvious in that they all know what they want, and, as one voice, they ask for **it** with one heart. They prayed in agreement for their **it** because they all longed for the same thing. They were extremely focused in their praying and not scattered. Their unity in prayer was a constant, and unity grew out of a common desire and a common desperateness (the cry of the Jews in Esther 4; the prayer of the church in Acts 4).

Ask and **it** *shall be given you; seek, and ye shall find* (implying that the **it** you are seeking will be the **it** you will find); *knock, and* **it** *shall be opened unto you.* (Matthew 7:6-8) I have heard John Franklin, author and public speaker on prayer and revival, say on numerous occasions that 37 times Jesus said, *Ask.* Evidently He wants us to ask, would you not agree? Every time we are told to ask, the focus is on an **it** or on something in particular. We have not begun to ask until we have an **it**. There has to be something on our heart and not just on our lips. He does not delight in us drawing near unto Him with our lips and honoring Him with our mouths, but He draws near to all who draw near unto Him with their heart. My fear is that we rarely come with an **it** on our heart. My experience is that we spend a lot of time praying for other people's **it** and rarely make their **it** ours, much less share our true **it**. There has to be a lot of trust and openness for individuals to share their **it** with others. Remember, **it** is your heart cry and is deeply personal.

Asking is at the very basic level of praying. The person has something they desire but they cannot obtain it on their own; that is why they ask. This person has come to the conclusion that their **it** is impossible if God does not intervene. They are not simply going through the motion of asking and then going off to make it happen. They realize God is their only hope. At the very basic level of asking, the person must confess he has a need he cannot resolve and needs divine help. He must humble himself and ask for divine intervention. This is very difficult for the American man who is taught not to ask for anything or for help with anything because doing so they believe would be a sign of weakness. That is the whole point; God wants man to admit he is weak and cannot do all things. We have a tendency to think, and even say, it is me and God. No, true prayer is God alone.

At the asking level of praying we must admit that it is God and God alone. I believe this is why most men do not ask for themselves but ask for others. When men do ask for something it is generally done so by offering God their help. Many men have a problem with being dependent upon anyone, even on God. The Greek word most often used for asking in Scripture conveys the idea of a request from a lesser to a greater. God did not choose the word used between two equals on purpose. God loves to answer prayers that give all the glory to Him. He does not seek to share His glory with man. He loves to reveal His glory to man and there is no better way for Him to do that than when He has a man saying, "Lord, I can't but you can. Help!" This man has humbled himself and is in a position for God to do a God-thing.

To ask in this way requires a confession, I cannot do this but God can. This goes deeper than saying, I need help; it simply cries, help! When we arrive at this level of asking, we are ready to hand **it** over to God because we know we have no hold on **it** any more, if we ever did. I believe most of the direct commands to ask and to pray are directed toward men because of this very point. God is not a male chauvinist, He delights in the prayers of all of His children, but He knows getting men to ask in this way requires more prompting and encouraging than it does for women or children. My experience has proven this to be so, hasn't yours? Men will pray, but rarely for themselves, and if they do, they have to be pretty desperate or broken. Pride and self-confidence must fade if one is going to even reach the very basic level of prayer whereby you ask in this way.

Ask and it shall be given you. Do you have an **it**? Do you have an **it** for your family? Do you have an **it** for your church? What is the one thing you long for God to do in your life, in your family, in your church, in your nation?

God is waiting for you to ask Him for your **it**. He certainly has communicated that desire through His Word. Don't keep Him waiting on you.

EXAMPLES OF "IT PRAYING" IN SCRIPTURE

I thought I would spur your interest by giving you a few examples of **it** prayers from Scripture. Perhaps as you study the Word of God, you will be on the lookout for some of your own. You will notice I have not included the prayers of Jesus or of Paul in this chapter; those will be dealt with in a later chapter.

ABRAHAM'S PRAYER FOR SODOM

And Abraham drew near, and said, 'Wilt thou also destroy the righteous with the wicked?' (Genesis 18:23) The rest of his pleas can be found in verses 24-33.

What was Abraham's **it** prayer?

ABRAHAM'S ELDEST SERVANT'S PRAYER

And he said, O LORD God of my master Abraham, I pray thee, send me good speed this day, and shew kindness unto my master Abraham. Behold, I stand here by the well of water; and the daughters of the men of the city come out to draw water: And let it come to pass, that the damsel to whom I shall say, Let down thy pitcher, I pray thee, that I may drink; and she shall say, Drink, and I will give thy camels drink also: let the same be she that thou hast appointed for thy servant Isaac; and thereby shall I know that thou hast shewed kindness unto my master. (Genesis 24:12-14)

The cry for help is always a good prayer, don't you agree? Did you underline his **it**?

A FEW OF MOSES' PRAYERS

And when the people complained, it displeased the LORD: and the LORD heard it; and his anger was kindled; and the fire of the LORD burnt among them, and consumed them that were in the uttermost parts of the camp. And the people cried unto Moses; and when Moses prayed unto the LORD, the fire was quenched. (Numbers 11:1-2) Would you agree that it is obvious Moses was probably very specific in what he asked the Lord to do? Do you think he was asking for a sunny day? Probably not. His **it** probably was reflective of the people's need. Does your **it** reflect the people's need?

And Moses cried unto the Lord, saying, Heal her now, O God, I beseech thee. (Numbers 12:13) Miriam and Aaron have been speaking against Moses because of the woman he has married. Leprosy consumes Miriam by the hand of the Lord. Moses turns to the Lord and pleas for her to be healed. A close look at the words of this verse reveals a very strong sense of urgency in Moses prayer. Moses' **it** is clear: he wants healing for his sister and he wants it now. It is not unusual for the **it** prayers to carry with them a great sense of urgency. Do yours?

Pardon, I beseech thee, the iniquity of this people according unto the greatness of thy mercy, and as thou hast forgiven this people, from Egypt even until now. And the Lord said, I have pardoned according to thy word: (Numbers 14:19-20) The prayer actually begins in verse 13 of this chapter, but it is obvious what Moses' **it** is for the people. This is not the first time he has asked for this **it,** and it won't be the last. Moses loved the people and he expressed that love in his **it** prayers for them. Do your prayers reflect your love?

Therefore the people came to Moses, and said, We have sinned, for we have spoken against the LORD, and against thee; pray unto the Lord, that he take away the serpents from us. And Moses prayed for the people. (Numbers 21:7) For what do you think he prayed?

Let me leave this one verse from Psalms with you concerning Moses and his prayers. *Therefore he said that he would destroy them, had not Moses his chosen stood before him in the breach, to turn away his wrath, lest he should destroy them.* (Psalm 106:23) Moses did this over and over again for his people. He was constantly asking God to forgive them and to have mercy on them. There aren't too many Moses types today. Perhaps that is part of our problem. When you love the people you are called to lead, you find yourself praying more for them than for yourself.

A PRAYER OF GIDEON

And he said unto him, If now I have found grace in thy sight, then shew me a sign that thou talkest with me. (Judges 6:17)

Gideon needed some clarity. He did not want to act without certainty; there was too much at stake. He saw himself as one of the least of Israel and the calling seemed too big for someone of humble birth. His **it** was for clarity. Have you ever needed clarity? What did you ask for? What was your **it** at that time?

HANNAH'S PRAYER FOR A BOY

And she was in bitterness of soul, and prayed unto the LORD, and wept sore. And she vowed a vow, and said, O LORD of hosts, if thou wilt indeed look on the affliction of thine handmaid, and remember me, and not forget thine handmaid, but wilt give unto thy handmaid a man child, then I will give him unto the LORD all the days of his life, and there shall no razor come upon his head. (I Samuel 1:10-11)

Did you notice how she prayed? How is her praying for her **it** described? Praying for your **it** is rarely a tissue-less event.

THE PRAYER OF JABEZ

And Jabez called on the God of Israel, saying, Oh that thou wouldest bless me indeed, and enlarge my coast, and that thine hand might be with me, and that thou wouldest keep me from evil, that it may not grieve me! And God granted him that which he requested. (I Chronicles 4:10)

The prayer of Jabez has gotten a lot of attention through the years and some have misunderstood his prayer and thus misused it. It is important to remember that in verse 9 God calls him *more honourable than his brethren.* There was a very distinct uniqueness about Jabez and his walk with the Lord. His prayer was reflective, not just a reflection of his faith but also of his relationship with God. I often remind people at the time of Jabez God's people have almost surrendered all of the land God had given them through the hand of Joshua back to their enemies. Jabez is very much like Joshua and Caleb, he is simply asking for God to give him what was already promised but which had been surrendered to the enemy. God found a man that wanted what He wanted and so the prayer is answered. The prayer of Jabez is not so much a prayer about bless me, as it is, Lord, I want what you want! When God's **it** becomes our **it,** you can count on something happening. What coasts and boundaries have you surrendered to the enemy you need to be asking back?

A PRAYER OF SOLOMON

Give me now wisdom and knowledge, that I may go out and come in before this people: for who can judge this thy people, that is so great? (II Chronicles 1:10)

This is not the only prayer of Solomon but it is the most well known. Solomon could have asked for many things but he chose to ask for one thing, the thing he needed most: wisdom. This was his **it**. Have you ever needed wisdom? Have you ever asked for it? God invites us just as he did Solomon to ask Him for wisdom. (James 1:5) He also promises to give us wisdom in abundance when we ask in faith. (James 1:5-6) **It** prayers should always be prayed in faith. Do you need wisdom?

A PRAYER OF ASA

And Asa cried unto the LORD his God, and said, LORD, it is nothing with thee to help, whether with many, or with them that have no power: help us, O LORD our God; for we rest on thee, and in thy name we go against this multitude. O LORD, thou art God; let no man prevail against thee. (II Chronicles 14:11)

Asa was a man that was either all for God or all against Him. There was no in between for him. He lived the first part of his life giving all for God and the last of his life fighting against God. Early in his reign he said a powerful prayer that had powerful results. I have included this prayer because this prayer is common in Scripture. As you search the Scriptures in the days ahead you will find it often. In this prayer there is one thing on the heart of the person of prayer: Help! There is some kind of present danger or threat. The greatness of this prayer is not in the prayer but in God's response. Our

God is the God of Psalm 46:1-2. He loves to respond to us when we turn to Him and Him alone. Read some of the cries of Psalms: 38:22; 56:9; 79:9. Are you in need of His help? He waits for you to ask.

THE PRAYER OF EZRA AND THE PEOPLE

Then I proclaimed a fast there, at the river of Ahava, that we might afflict ourselves before our God, to seek of him a right way for us, and for our little ones, and for all our substance. (Ezra 8:21)

What was their **it**? Why do you think God's Word describes them praying for their **it** with the words *afflict ourselves*? What do you think that looked like?

A PRAYER OF NEHEMIAH

And it came to pass, that when I heard these words, that I sat down and wept, and mourned certain days, and fasted, and prayed before the God of heaven, (Nehemiah 1:4)

Would you agree Nehemiah was desperate? To find his **it** you have to read on. I challenge you to read his prayer and the rest of Nehemiah. You will find Nehemiah was not a man slow to plea for his **it**. Nehemiah is a man of prayer, and he is always quick to reveal his **it** when he prays. Are you?

THE PRAYERS OF DAVID

David's prayers are too numerous to list here but each one reveals his **it** of the hour. When Nathan rebukes him for his sins with Bathsheba, he pleads for the life of his newborn son. In Psalm 51 he pleads for cleansing of his sins and a restoration of his joy. Throughout the Psalms he states his **it** of the hour before the Lord. My challenge to you is to put this book down, turn to the Psalms, and listen to the **its** of David. You will see David was always very clear about what he longed for from the Lord. May we always be as clear.

A PRAYER OF JOB

And the Lord turned the captivity of Job, when he prayed for his friends:

also the LORD gave Job twice as much as he had before. (Job 42:10)

There are many prayers in the book of Job but this one prayer ends the book and ends his misery. But it is not a prayer we would anticipate knowing the situation that Job is in. These friends of Job have not spoken anything right about Job. For days they have told him he must have sinned in some major way. They tell him to confess it and come clean before God. The problem is, they are wrong and they now have evoked the wrath of God upon themselves. God has told them unless they go to Job and ask him to pray for them they will not have a chance before God. What a humbling thing they are called upon to do. These men who have all of their possessions and all of their health must go to one who has neither of these things and ask him to pray for them. Job, on the other hand, is still covered with sores, he is still in great pain, his children are still dead, he has lost everything. In other words, his situation has not changed. Yet he must pray for these who are well and wealthy. Job does not hesitate or complain, he prays for them and then something unexpected happens. You see, he is praying for these men so you would expect the next verse would say something like this, the friends of Job were spared the wrath of God when Job prayed for them. But the surprise is that when Job prays for his friends something happens to Job. Job's captivity is turned. The **it** of Job's prayer was not for himself but for his friends, yet God does something for Job. Often it is the case that when praying for others' **its**, God grants to us our **it**.

PRAYERS OF THE PROPHETS

There is not enough space to cover all of the prophets' **its**, but, if we were to do so, we would discover the prophets' **its** were reflections of the prophecies they were given. Each prayed according to what they had heard from God. In Isaiah 6, Isaiah hears that God is looking for someone to go for Him to the people and what does Isaiah pray, *Send me.* Elijah is told there will be no rain for the people of God, and, so, what does he pray, *Lord shut off the rain!* Three years later, he is told it is time for rain, and, so, what does he pray, *Lord send rain!* On that same day, he stands before the false prophets of Baal and King Ahab and prays, *Lord show them that I have done all* *these things by your word. Show them that I am your servant. Consume this sacrifice by fire!*

And so it is that the prophets asked for the **it** that was on the heart of God at that time. Why? Because that was what was on their heart as well. I am going to make a statement you may not agree with, but hear me out. Who is in the best position to pray the will of God? Is it not the one whom God has revealed His will to? Well then, who is in the best position to pray before the Word is preached or when the Word is taught? Is it not the one whom God has prepared to preach or teach at that time? They know what God wants to say to His people better than anyone else at that time, and so they are in the best position to reflect the heart of God in their prayers. The prophets were in the best position to pray for the people of God when a prophecy came because of the fact they first had received that prophecy. Do your prayers reflect what God has said to you?

THE PRAYER OF THE PUBLICAN

God be merciful to me a sinner. (Luke 18:13b)

In a parable Jesus records the prayer of a Publican, a known sinner. This man comes into the temple and begins to pray. He only wants one thing, he only has one **it**: Mercy! He beats his chest and he lowers his head. His body language makes it clear he knows what he needs and is desperate for what he needs. What is his **it**? Mercy! I know I just said that, but, do you understand it is rare for a man to want mercy and mercy alone. We don't know if he just found out that he is about to die. If that had been the case, then we may understand this request. Something has stirred his heart to come to a place he normally doesn't come to. Something has caused him to act the way he does. Something has caused him to ask for what he does. What would cause a grown man to come to a public place and beat himself and beg for mercy? What would cause this to become the **it** of any man? The Spirit of God and the conviction thereof is the only thing that would cause a man to behave as he does. His **it** is for himself, and it is his **it** God grants. He finds mercy. Do you remember having this **it**?

THE CHALLENGE TO PRAY FOR WISDOM

In times when we find ourselves overcome by trials and temptations and struggling to understand what God is doing in the midst of it all, we are directed to ask for one thing: Wisdom. *If any of you lack wisdom, let him ask of God, that giveth to all men liberally, and upbraideth not; and it shall be given him.* (James 1:5) That which God promises to provide to the one who asks for wisdom is wisdom. I do not know how many times I have prayed this prayer, and, how many times I have joined others in praying for this. Some add wisdom to their daily list of desires but it is not sought with any more intensity than anything else on their list. But the person directed to pray for this **it** is different, this person feels overwhelmed by his situation and desperately wants some light in his darkness. When he prays for wisdom, he does so with great longing. He desperately wants some understanding.

Do you remember a time when wisdom, truth, and light in the midst of your darkness were all you longed for? Do you remember a time when you just wanted to know why? This was the prayer of Habakkuk (Habakkuk 1:2-3). It was the cry of Ezra in the travel to the promise land. It is the cry of Job. The challenge God makes to His children that lack understanding is to ask Him. He makes a powerful encouraging promise to answer them with more than they can comprehend. It is God that invites us to have this **it** in His presence in times of trials and temptation.

THE LAST PRAYER OF SCRIPTURE

Even the last prayer of Scripture is a single focused prayer. Listen to Revelation 22:17, *And the Spirit and the bride say, Come. And let him that heareth say, Come. And let him that is athirst come. And whosoever will, let him take the water of life freely.*

The church is to join the Spirit in praying come! That is an **it** prayer. It is to be our final cry. It is the cry of the Spirit, and it should be the cry of the church. Someone said to me, "I struggle in praying that prayer. If he comes now there will be so many that will go to hell." I said to him, "The population of the world is growing at an alarming rate, the number of believers are shrinking. Every moment Jesus waits there are more and more lost and less and less believers." He immediately understood. The last prayer of Scripture is an **it** prayer. Have you joined the Spirit in this prayer? Have you been obedient to this challenge to the Church?

The Scriptures are filled with prayers that reflect the desire of God's people. I challenge you to discover them and see how your prayers and the prayers of your church measure up in comparison. As you listen to the Word of God preached and taught, see if you can discover the heart cry, the **it** of the passage. As you have your quiet time, try to create a sensitivity to hearing the **its** of the people of God in Scripture. As you listen to prayer requests at your church, listen for the **its** of your brothers and sisters in Christ. Take a simple journey, a mission of discovery by starting in Genesis and ending up in Revelation. Take the time to read and to mark the **its** of the recorded prayers of Scripture. You will learn much about the heart of God's people as you do so.

4

GOD'S ITS

Matthew 7:7 should be interpreted in light of its context. It is not an invitation to pray for your **it,** but a challenge to pray for God's **it.** In the Sermon on the Mount Jesus has a very specific audience in mind—His disciples. (Matthew 5:1-2) This message was to them, and it was about what Jesus expects of those who follow Him. Matthew 6:9-13 records what is commonly known as the Lord's Prayer, but it is clearly a prayer that Jesus calls His disciples to pray. In this prayer He records what He desires for them to ask for—the kingdom of God. At first glance this prayer appears to have many **its,** but a closer look reveals all the requests are connected to one primary **it,** the kingdom of God. His kingdom is a holy kingdom and, thus, where His kingdom is, His name is hallowed. His kingdom has one king, and, where there is one king, there is only one will that is done: His! In His kingdom, subjects rely on Him to provide the supplies they need to do His will. They are directed to ask Him for their daily provisions so they may hallow His name and do His will. We cannot do His will without His fresh provisions. We *can do all things through Christ which strengthens* us (Philippians 4:13), but *apart from Him we can do nothing* (John 15:5). A crucial part to His name being hallowed and His kingdom being evident in our lives is that we are quick to forgive others and to seek forgiveness for ourselves. His kingdom does not allow for any other kings or lords in our lives, so He invites us to ask Him to deliver us from evil. If He is our King then we will desire for Him to lead us. Why are we to ask for these things? Because it is all about His kingdom, His power, and His glory! We are His subjects, His children.

God's **it** is the kingdom of God. Before He gives us Matthew 7:7, He tells us to ask for the kingdom. We should never become so focused in asking for our **it** that we fail to ask for His **it.** This is even clearer as we continue through chapter 6. He ends this chapter by encouraging us to not become so anxious about our **it** we fail to seek His **it.** What is His **it** we are to seek? That's right—the kingdom of God and His righteousness. So the **it** to be sought in Matthew 7:7 is first His **it** and not ours. Never are we to seek our **it** above His. He makes an incredible promise in Matthew 6:33 … if we will seek His kingdom and His righteousness (His **it**) He will add unto us what? *All these things*. What things? Matthew 6:19-32 deals with the other things, the very things that generally become our **its**. Things like wealth, power, things of life, and basic needs (food, drink, clothing, housing, the very things that Gentiles seek). In other words, lost people are concerned about these things, but we have a different relationship with Him than they do. We know our Father and know He is concerned about us. He will take care of those things. If we seek His **it,** then He makes a promise to add all these other things unto us. He makes no promise to add the kingdom and His righteousness unto us if we seek our **it** over His **it**. But if we will seek His **it,** then we better stand back because He has a promise that is on the way. *All these things* are only added to those who seek first His kingdom and His righteousness.

We are called to be kingdom citizens. We each have a unique calling but we all strive for a common purpose—the kingdom of God. My calling is my contribution to the kingdom; my calling is not the kingdom. In fact, the kingdom of God is bigger than anyone's calling. It is bigger than any time period and is not tied to any church or denomination. It is God-sized and not man-sized. In the overall context of the Sermon on the Mount, the knocking would relate to the kingdom being opened unto us. God's **it** in the Gospels is His kingdom. Jesus came to fulfill His Father's **it**.

God's will is always bigger than you and me, and it is always bigger than our **it**, but isn't it beautiful that we have a God who cares about us and our **it**? Because He cares for us, He cares for our **it**, and we ought to be a people who care for His **it**. So, as you pray, never fail to ask Him what His **it** is in the midst of every situation. Often you will find that when you start asking for His **it,** your **it** will change.

God has taken the time to reveal His **it** to us. He even tells us what to pray. He has written them down and has called us to pray for them. He waits for us to do so. What an incredible thought. When we are praying the Lord's Prayer, we are asking for what He desires. Many of us know if we ask anything according to His will, we know He hears us and we have it. (1

John 5:14-15) Praying for the things He has told us to pray for should be a no brainer for us, but we seem to be persistent in creating our own prayers instead of praying what He told us to pray. His **it** is revealed in the cries of His Son. As children of the King, our cries should reflect His cries.

God's **its** have eternal significance while ours, on the other hand, are often very temporal. God invites us to join Him in His work of hallowing His name and seeing His kingdom come and His will be done. His **its** are bigger than the present and bigger than any person or situation. When we join Him in His **its,** we find ourselves praying prayers that have been uttered since the beginning of time. When we pray His **its,** we are never the first to do so. Our cry is added to a great cloud of witnesses and prayer warriors who prayed with all their hearts, even to death, for His **its**. For example, think of the last prayer of Scripture, *Come quickly Lord Jesus come*! (Revelation 22:20) Can we even imagine how many have cried that prayer? I think not. How many gave their life praying that prayer? How many times has our Lord heard that cry, yet He has called His people to keep praying it as though we were the first to do so. Is God answering that request? Yes! He answered that prayer by coming into my life and into yours, and, one day, He is going to come again for the whole world to see and know!

What an incredible privilege God has extended to us by inviting us to ask for what He longs to do. What an incredible sacred trust He has bestowed upon us that He would even delight in hearing from us about anything much less about His kingdom. Accept this holy, sacred trust and begin today to pray the prayers He has told us to pray. May we be found asking for His **it**. Are you? Have you been so concerned for your **it**, you have failed to ask for His? Never put your **it** above His for at that moment you are no longer *seeking first His kingdom and His righteousness*.

JESUS' ITS

I am constantly reminding myself that God never wastes a single word. (He is not like me. It takes me way too many words to express myself, and when I'm done, there is still more that should have been said.) This is true when it comes to prayer as well. Unlike our ramblings in prayer,

Jesus knows exactly what to pray and never prays wrong. His prayers are very specific and always on target. Jesus loves to direct others to join Him in His praying. I am convinced one of the reasons God records prayers is because He is inviting us to join them in their praying. Our Lord is not only one who intercedes for us, but He also invites us to join Him in His intercession.

The prayers of Jesus reflect the **its** of His Father. He doesn't pray with multiple choice prayers. Jesus knows the heart and will of the Father, and He reflects those in His prayers. Jesus came to finish the work the Father assigned to Him. He knew His purpose, and He never did anything prematurely. Everything was done in order and on time. He made no errors in anything He did. Jesus did the will of the Father perfectly, and He prayed the will of the Father perfectly. He does not fill His prayers with tons of words and does not hesitate to ask for something more than once (His prayer in the garden). He never prayed wrong. His prayers were a reflection of His heart which was in perfect tune with the heart of the Father. So in all of His prayers, His teachings on prayer, and in His prayer directives, you find the perfect will of God. A word of clarification is in order at this point. The Scriptures record the prayers of Jesus, His teachings on prayer, and His prayer directives. Prayer directives are what some might call prayer requests, but they actually are much stronger than that. A prayer request is left open. For example, pray for me I have cancer. We do not know what to pray for, it is assumed that healing is what is being requested but in a prayer request we are not told exactly what to pray for. A prayer directive, on the other hand, is very specific in who is being asked to pray and for what is being told to pray for. For example, the Lord's Prayer is a prayer directive of Jesus. We are told who is to pray it and what is exactly to be asked for. We will take a look at both of these, but let's begin with a few of the actual prayers of Jesus.

The first actual recorded prayer of Jesus is found in Matthew 11:25 (there are many prayer directives given by Jesus to His disciples, but this is His first actual recorded prayer), and it is a prayer of thanks. Jesus has a very specific **it** for which He gives thanks. He thanks the Father for hiding the things of the kingdom from the wise and prudent but revealing them unto babes. This prayer is very similar to the prayer of praise Jesus offers in Luke 10 where He also lets His disciples know they are blessed because they have seen what many prophets and kings have longed to see. Perhaps not what we would be praising God for, but, then again, we aren't God and do not know the heart and will of God like Jesus did. This prayer of gratitude may sound strange to us, but this truth is often revealed or stated in the Gospels.

The second prayer in Matthew is also a prayer of thanks or blessing and is found in the feeding of the 5,000 (14:15-21). The prayer itself is not recorded, but again the prayer is very specific in nature. He blesses the loaves and fish. The idea of a blessing on the food is much more than what is the norm today. Blessings in the mind of the Jews were primarily reserved for God's people. A blessing was rarely used solely for a thing. The thing was blessed so it could become a blessing for the people. This prayer is immediately answered and this blessing enlarges the supply so as to provide for a vast multitude. He asked, and it was done. Blessings in Scripture were reserved for people, and things were only blessed in order to be a blessing for people. We would do good to remember this. (The event of feeding the 4,000 in Matthew 15:32-39 reveals the same pattern.) The prayers of thanks and blessings are common in the life of Jesus. He is found giving thanks for provisions (loaves and fish, bread and cup) and asks the Father to bless them. The blessings are requests for the Father to increase or multiply or to use them in order for people to be blessed so the kingdom of God could advance.

Matthew 19:13-15 records little children being brought to Him for prayer, though the prayers are not recorded, the intent is—God's favor on the children. Though we do not know what Jesus prayed for each of these children, we do know He did pray for them. He did so by laying His hands on each of them implying each prayer was a personal prayer just for that child. Wouldn't you have liked to have been there to hear what He prayed for in the life of each child? What do you think He would ask for in the life of your child or grandchild?

In Luke 11:13 Jesus makes a prayer promise that reveals a very clear **it** of His for us. *If ye then, being evil, know how to give good gifts unto your children: how much more shall your heavenly Father give the Holy Spirit to them* *that ask Him?* The Father is waiting for us to ask for the Holy Spirit, that is an **it** desire of His heart.

Matthew describes Jesus in prayer in the garden with words that are so intense, descriptive, and emotional many have been able to paint pictures of the scene. Listen to some of the words: "He began to be sorrowful and very heavy"; "my soul is exceeding sorrowful, even unto death"; "He fell on His face". Matthew records His agony and not just His prayer. The Holy Spirit, in the inspiration of this, wanted us to know this prayer was an expression of His physical, emotional, mental, and spiritual state. He has only one true cry: *Thy will be done.* (Matthew 26:42) It is a prayer of surrender and not a prayer of searching. The prayer, *If it be your will* is intended to be more a prayer of surrender to His will than a prayer searching for His will. In Scripture, this prayer comes from an individual who knows what the will of God is and is ready for it to be done. It is a cry that says, Let it be.

The selection of the 12 was only after a night of prayer. (Luke 6:12-13) Though the actual prayer is not revealed, it is apparent He was seeking direction as to who the apostles should be.

In Luke 22:31-34, Jesus tells us the purpose of the prayer. Sometimes the English language is inadequate and can actually cause us to miss an important revelation. This text holds one of those pearls that is often overlooked because of the English language. This is one of those verses that should be read either in the Greek or in the King James Version. Why? Let me show you. Listen to verse 31 and 32 as it appears in the King James Version. *And the Lord said, Simon, Simon, behold, Satan hath desired to have you, that he may sift you as wheat: But I have prayed for thee, that thy faith fail not: and when thou art converted, strengthen thy brethren.* Did you see the pearl, the truth is hidden in other translations? Probably not. I didn't either at first until I saw the Greek and then remembered a secret of the King James Version. Here is the secret (not so secret by the way) of the King James Version: y's are plural and t's are singular. Now what does that mean? In the old English, when two or more persons are being addressed, you, ye or your were used, and, when one individual was being addressed, thee, thou or thine were used. With that in mind, listen to this passage again and listen for the y's and the t's.

And the Lord said, Simon, Simon, behold, Satan hath desired to have you (you all: meaning all of the disciples), *that he may sift you* (you all) *as wheat: But I have prayed for thee* (Simon), *that thy* (Simon's) *faith fail not: and when thou* (Simon) *art converted, strengthen thy* (Simon's) *brethren.* Do you see it now? Satan is going to sift all of them, but Jesus does not pray for all of them, He prays only for Peter! This is not the sifting of Peter but of the disciples. Why doesn't Jesus pray for all of them if He knows all of them are going to be sifted by Satan? What would you have prayed? This is one of the main differences between Jesus and us. We would say, "Why not, I mean, if we are going to pray for one, why not for the whole?" That is the whole point, Jesus never prays wrong, and He doesn't just throw out a bunch of options for God in prayer. Jesus always prays right and never wastes a word. Every word is handpicked. Listen, as far as Jesus is concerned, the best way to pray for the whole is to pray specifically for Peter. At this point, Jesus' **it** is not the deliverance of Peter. He could have asked that satan not sift them at all, but, instead, He prays for the faith of Peter not to fail. Why only Peter's faith? Jesus knows the Father has chosen Peter to be the instrument to strengthen the faith of the whole. So Jesus prays for Peter, and, in so doing, He is praying for the best for the whole. That is why, after He has prayed for Peter, He commissions him to strengthen the others. And Peter does! Acts has Peter doing just that, strengthening the brethren. Do you see the importance of knowing the will of God when you pray? This knowledge should shape our praying and our **its**. It did Jesus. Does it yours?

One of the most amazing prayers from the cross is, *…Father, forgive them; for they know not what they do. …* (Luke 23:34) What a prayer of grace! It cries of the **it** of Christ, for He came to die and to forgive. This is His heart cry, this is His desire—men might be forgiven. The prayer takes on incredible significance when you realize it comes not from the manger but from the cross. They have done incredible, horrible things to Him, and, yet, He pleads for forgiveness. Did they know what they were doing? No, they might have known they were persecuting and killing an innocent man, but they did not know this man was the only Son of God, their only hope for salvation. They did not know He was the only way to the Father. They knew nothing of His greatness; they only saw a man or a prophet. But it didn't matter if they knew, Jesus still prayed for them to be forgiven. What an **it**! I have heard this **it** from missionaries for the people they are called to reach and from others who had people they loved and longed to be saved. Have you ever joined Jesus in praying this **it**? Do you have someone you long for the Father to forgive?

... Father, into thy hands I commend my spirit: ... (Luke 23:46) Now that is a prayer of surrender, wouldn't you agree? No more requests, just a gift, a gift for you and me. One thing, and, only one thing, He prays in this prayer, one thing He offers—His life. Paul, Moses and others wanted to give their life for their people, but they could not. Others have died so others could live, but only one died so all men could live forever. Now that is a prayer that gives all. Wouldn't you agree?

According to the Gospel of Luke, Jesus departs after His resurrection only after He has prayed a prayer of blessing on the disciples, a prayer with one purpose, a prayer for their good, and a prayer of blessing. The prayers of blessing were common in the life of the patriarchs. They expressed what they longed for God to do in the life of their children. Jesus, like the patriarchs of old, lifted up His hand and blessed them. Just like He had the loaves and the fish, like the bread and the cup, and like the little children they wanted to send away. He blessed them. He asked for the Father's good to be realized in their lives. Now that is a good **it**.

There are other times in the Gospels where Jesus is said to be praying, but the exact prayer is not recorded. But when they are, the pattern remains the same. He prays with purpose and clarity for the will of the Father.

Do you reflect the **its** of the Father and Jesus in your prayers? Does your church's prayers reflect the **its** of God? One of the reasons we are given the intercession work of the Holy Spirit is because we (the Church) do not know what we should pray for as we ought. But the Holy Spirit, like Jesus, always prays according to the will of God (Romans 8:26-34), and we are called upon to strive to do the same. (I John 5:14-15) Our prayers should sound like theirs. Do your prayers sound like theirs? Does your church's prayers sound like theirs? Isn't it about time we joined them in their praying rather than trying to get them to join us?

5

SHEPHERDING GOD'S PEOPLE TO PRAY FOR "IT"

In May 1774 the British Parliament had ordered an embargo on the Port of Boston, Massachusetts, effective June 1. The following was a resolution recorded in the "Journals of The House of Burgesses of Virginia," 1773-1776, edited by John Pendleton Kennedy.

Tuesday, the 24th of May, 14 Geo. III. 1774

> This House, being deeply impressed with Apprehension of the great Dangers, to be derived to British America, from the hostile Invasion of the City of Boston, in our Sister Colony of Massachusetts Bay, whose Commerce and Harbour are, on the first Day of June next, to be stopped by an armed Force, deem it highly necessary that the said first Day of June be set apart, by the Members of this House, as a Day of Fasting, Humiliation, and Prayer, devoutly to implore the Divine Interposition, for averting the heavy Calamity which threatens Destruction to our civil Rights, and the Evils of civil War; to give us one Heart and one Mind to oppose, by all just and proper Means, every Injury to American Rights…

> Ordered, therefore, that the Members of this House do attend in their Places, at the Hour of ten in the forenoon, on the said first Day of June next, in order to proceed with the Speaker, and the Mace, to the Church in this City, for the Purposes aforesaid; and that the Reverend Mr. Price be appointed to read Prayers, and the Reverend Mr. Gwatkin, to preach a Sermon, suitable to the Occasion.

George Washington wrote in his diary for the first day of June, "Went to Church and fasted all Day." (This information can be found in Dereck Prince's book, <u>Shaping History through Prayer and Fasting</u>, Whitaker House, New Kensington, PA, pages 185-187.)

The truth is many American presidents have called our nation to prayer that had a very clear **it.** Abraham Lincoln on several occasions called our nation to prayer during the Civil War. John Adams proclaimed a day of solemn assembly on May 9, 1798 due to the threat of war with France. The call to prayer he issued was very precise, *That it be made the subject of particular and earnest supplication, that our country may be protected from all the dangers which threaten it: That our civil and religious privileges may be preserved inviolate, and perpetuated to the latest generation...*" (Appendix no. 7, Volume 11, U.S. Statutes At Large)

January 12, 1815 was set aside as a day of prayer and fasting by James Madison and the House of Congress due to war with Britain. The prayer was, *Prayer to Almighty God for the safety and welfare of these States, his blessings on their arms and a speedy restoration of peace.* (Appendix no. 14, Volume 11, U.S. Statutes At Large)

In chapter 8 of **Early Tennessee Baptists** by O. W. Taylor (copyrighted 1957), there is a record of years of corporate calls to prayer and fasting that ushered in the Great Revival of 1800. These calls to prayer and fasting were **it** driven.

> The minutes of the body record that Elkhorn Baptist Association in Kentucky, meeting at Bryan's Station in October, 1793, in response to a request of the church at Columbia, set aside a specific date as 'a day of fasting and humiliation before God for the preservation and success of our Army against the Enemy and for the suppression of Vice in our land' and directed that a copy of the action be sent to Christians of other denominations 'hoping they will join us in our petition.' Also in August, 1795, at Cooper's Run, Elkhorn: 'Agreed to recommend to the Churches to set apart the 2nd Saturday in September as a day of fasting and prayer to implore the divine blessing upon our state and upon the Churches that the Lord would bless his own institution of a preached Gospel that he would check the rapid spread of impiety and infidelity.' (152-153)

> As early as the year 1778, a revival was greatly desired, and a fast was proclaimed, to humble ourselves before the Lord, and to so-

licit the throne of grace for a revival. In 1785, at Shoulder's Hill, another fast was proclaimed. The same year, at an Association at Kehukee, it was agreed to set apart some time between sun-set and dark every day, for all the churches to unite together in prayer, and earnestly pray for a revival. And in 1794, the Association agreed to appoint the Saturday before the fourth Sunday in every month, a day of prayer meetings throughout the churches; whereon all the members of the respective churches were requested to meet at their meeting-houses, or places of worship, and there for each of them, as far as time would permit, to make earnest prayer and supplication to Almighty God for a revival of religion. (153)

This was a description of the call to prayer by the Kehukee Association in North Carolina.

For nearly 15 years leading up to the Great Revival of 1800 Baptists, Methodists, Dutch Reform, Presbyterians and others called their people to focused, earnest prayers for revival. This was **it** praying at a corporate level. These men and women of God did not hesitate to call the people of God to focused, intentional prayer. They did not spend these days in many prayers but in prayers with one purpose in mind: Revival!

The evidence is clear in the biblical record as well that God used leaders to call His people to clear **it** prayers that resulted in revival, deliverance, and forgiveness on more than one event. The first Passover was a time of consecration for all the people of God. The focus was clear and the purpose was even clearer. Elijah on Mount Carmel challenged the people of God to dedicate themselves to the Lord and the Lord only. The book of Esther is a book about what God does as His people unite in prayer and fasting seeking His face to deliver them from the threat of annihilation. Prophets, kings, priests, and judges are recorded often calling the people of God to focus **it** praying. The situation changes as do the prayers, but God remains the same.

As a leader of God's people, we too are expected to call them to unified, one accord prayers when needful. A good and godly leader knows how to do so by learning from the godly leaders that have gone before him. We can learn much from the prayers of the biblical leaders. We can learn not only how to lead but how to lead others to pray. May this just be a beginning to your learning.

Romans 8:26-27 states, *Likewise the Spirit also helpeth our infirmities: for we know not what we should pray for as we ought: but the Spirit itself maketh intercession for us with groanings which cannot be uttered. And he that searcheth the hearts knoweth what is the mind of the Spirit, because he maketh intercession for the saints according to the will of God.* Let me call your attention to the statement, *for we know not what we should pray for as we ought.* One of the reasons why the Holy Spirit intercedes for us is because we do not know what we should for pray. The reason we don't know is because we have not sought to know. We often begin praying before we start asking for wisdom. God invites us to ask Him for wisdom about what He is doing in our lives. We are in a much better position to pray when we have first heard from Him. Another reason we do not know what we should pray for is because we have not obeyed the plea of Romans 12:1-2. We have failed to ... *present your bodies a living sacrifice, holy, acceptable unto God,* and have not sought to ... *be transformed by the renewing of your mind, that ye may prove what is that good, and acceptable, and perfect, will of God.*

Notice in Romans 8:27 the Holy Spirit prays only according to the will of God and not according to our will or even His will. We are taught in I John 5:14-15 that we can know our prayers are heard when we pray according to the will of God. Our challenge has always been to pray according to God's will and not ours. The reason the Spirit intercedes for us is because we do not pray for what we ought. In Romans 8:34 we are told Jesus also makes intercession for us. Now what do you think Jesus is praying for? The will of the Father! A simple reading of the Gospel of John makes it clear Jesus does nothing on His own but does the will of the Father. Doing the will of the Father is His meat; that satisfies Him.

NOTE: Romans 8:26-27 is in the plural; the word is **we** and not **I**. This refers to believers, the Church. The Church is given the gift of intercession of the Holy Spirit and the Son. Why? Because the Church does not know what it should pray for as it ought. That is something very different than "I do not know what to pray for as I ought." This is not a personal problem. It is a Church problem, but God has taken care of this problem by giving us the intercession of the Spirit and the Son. For this I am extremely grateful. But for this the CHURCH should be extremely grateful.

So the Spirit prays for us because we don't pray as we ought, which means we often pray wrong. Here is the question. If we only get our prayer requests from those who do not know what they should pray for as they ought, what kind of praying will we do? In other words, if we only ask those that He says do not know what they should pray for as they ought about what we should pray for, will we ever pray for what we ought to pray for? And the answer to that question? No. We will never begin to pray according to His will until we start getting our prayer directives from Him.

We have two sources for our prayer requests—the throne or the pew. Another way of stating it is— the Shepherd or the sheep. We spend most of our time getting our prayer requests from those who do not know what they should pray for. We rarely start prayer by asking Jesus what is on His heart or what is it He desires to happen in our present situation. We rarely ask the one who always prays correctly what we should be praying for. Instead, we ask those who don't know what to pray for about what we should pray for. We must strive to have our minds renewed by first presenting ourselves at the feet of God. We must at some point ask these simple questions—

Lord, what are you praying for in the midst of this situation?

Lord, what do you desire to see happen in me?

Lord, what should I be asking you for?

Lord, I need wisdom about what you are doing so my prayers, my requests, my thanks, my confessions, my petitions, and my intercessions reflect your will. Before we start asking for our **it,** we need to come to grips with His **it.** Often that means we must simply surrender to His will before we even know what it is. We are called upon to pray for one another and to minister to one another through prayer. However, our primary task is to see those we pray for surrender to the Lordship of Jesus in everything. This ultimately should become the goal of all prayer—asking for and yielding to the will of God.

Our Lord cares deeply for His sheep, and, thus, when we seek Him, He will always lead us back to the sheep. If we always get our requests from the sheep only, we may never get to the Shepherd. We have learned a method of prayer that seeks first the sheep and their desires. Thus, we keep asking those that do not know what they should pray for what we should pray for when we could be asking the one that always knows what we should be praying for. The Father loves His children and He knows what is best for each and every one of them. He waits for us to remember this and to cast all of our cares upon Him knowing His love will care for them as is best. We pray without an understanding of His will simply because we have started at the wrong source—our will instead of His. We say we are to seek Him first, but then we seek others first. We do not know the will of God unless we ask for it and seek it.

This is the first thing we are told to pray for in the midst of temptation and trials. James 1:5 encourages us to ask for wisdom when we lack it. We are to ask for this wisdom with two things settled—

- faith to believe He grants wisdom to all who ask
- once He speaks wisdom into our lives then He expects us not to be a hearer only but a doer also

Part of the doing is evident in the transformation of our prayers. When God grants wisdom about our situation, our prayers must reflect that wisdom. That is what happened when Paul was praying for his thorn to be removed. God spoke wisdom into his life and, thus, his prayer had to change. Our prayers should change when God grants wisdom to us. When we ask God to speak truth into our lives, we need to remember that God doesn't speak simply for informational purposes. God always speaks for transformational purposes. He doesn't speak just so we can know more, but so we can obey more. This is true in prayer as well. We need to first seek His face before we seek the face of others.

Whether alone in prayer or in a group, we need to ask, Lord what would you have me to pray for in this situation? What needs to be confessed? What do we need to give you praise and thanks for? What are the supplies we should be asking for? Those who lead God's people in prayer should always seek to lead God's people beyond where they are and beyond their requests to the Throne of God. The primary task is to lead others to God and not just to lead them in prayer. Those who lead others in prayer have a high calling of leading those same people to God. When one is leading others to God in prayer, those prayers will reflect the desires of God and not just the desires of those who are praying.

NOTE: Everything that comes out of the mouth comes from the heart. So what we pray for is a reflection of our heart. What are your prayers telling about your heart? If the will of God is what you desire, then your prayers will reflect both a seeking and a submission to His will.

Asking searching questions can often assist God's people to struggle with the will of God in their given situation.

1.) What is the one thing you believe God wants to do in your life?
2.) What is the one thing you believe God wants to do in your family?
3.) What is the one thing you believe God wants to do in your church in the midst of this?
4.) What do you think God is trying to do in the midst of your present situation?
5.) What of His will are you certain of in this situation?
6.) What has He revealed to you already about what He is doing in your life?
7.) What do you know He desires of you at all times and not just at this time?
8.) Is there something He is waiting for you to confess?
9.) Is there something He is waiting for you to yield to Him?
10.) Is He calling you? If so, how does this fit in that call and how should you be praying right now?
11.) What is His it?
12.) What should be your it?
13.) What should be our it?
14.) If you were to ask a Prayer Warrior to pray for one thing, what would it be?

Do you know what God's **it** is for your life? Do you know what God's **it** is for your church? Does your prayer life reflect His **it**? Do the prayers of your church reflect His **it**? Should you be praying for wisdom? You must be led by Him if you are going to be able to lead others to Him. Are you? Is this seen in your praying? Do your prayers reflect His **it** or just yours?

Before you can lead others to pray for the **it** of God, you must first have a heart for His **it**. You must long for His **it**. You must at least understand that His **it** will be in keeping with His revealed will in Scripture, the purpose of His Son, the life He expects all of His children to live, and in keeping with His personal call for your life. Shepherding God's people to pray for His **it** requires an understanding of what God is seeking among them. This is seen in the following examples. The prophets would often spend time pleading for the people because they had been shown the condition of the people and of God's discipline toward them. The 10 lepers were healed, but only one returned to give thanks. Why? Because he understood Jesus to be the hand of the Father at work in his life. Joel spends his time in prayers of lament because he has been given a glimpse of the great loss the people of God have suffered.

When you have heard from God, it empowers you to talk to Him in a way that reflects His heart and will. Have you heard from Him?

Before we leave this section, I want to challenge you to consider that in Scripture, and, in life, all prayer requests can fit into three categories: **Crisis**, **Calling**, and **Kingdom**. **Crisis** prayers are temporal, earthly, and, generally, very personal. **Crisis** prayers will always be because we live in a fallen world, a world that is passing and fading away. We live in a world that is decaying, dying, and rotting. Because of the fall of man, we, too, are like the earth. One crisis may pass, but there is always another on the way. These include all the things that cause us anxiety and fear. They include sickness, disease, famine, war, marital and family problems, storms, economical crisis, persecution, and well, I think you get the idea. These always carry with them a sense of nowness. But these are the very things Jesus spoke of in Matthew 6 when he said not to worry with them because the Father has these things. But we are also directed to pray for others in their times of distress, and we are challenged to cast our cares (whatever they may be) upon Him. Most of our prayer lists are filled with these kinds.

Calling requests reflect the mission and directives God's children have from Him. These are also very personal. Calling impacts the lives of those in this earthly realm as well as having heavenly significance. Our callings come from above and seek to direct others to look toward Him. Every believer has a calling. There is a universal element to our calling and a specific element. We are all called to fulfill the Great Commission and the Great Commandment. The call to hallow His name and to do His will are universal callings for all of God's children. But there is also a very specific calling for each of us. He has gifted and empowered us for our specific calling as well as for His universal calling. Most of the prayers of the New Testament, especially of Paul, reflect prayers are driven by God's calling in mind.

Kingdom requests are bigger than any man, any church, any denomination. They are not bound to any generation or any time period. They are not generated by us or even by the whole Church. These are kingdom requests because they come from the King himself. All we are to do is pray them. He has given them to us. He has had them recorded, and He waits for us to ask for them.

Now, most of what I hear our churches praying for fall into the crisis category. It is not that we are not aware of the others as it is that we choose to pray for what is on our hearts and not what is on His. What is on your heart comes out of your mouth. So if your heart is consumed with the present and the earthly, then your prayers will reflect that. If your heart is consumed with the heavenly and the eternal, then your prayers will reflect that reality.

I share this so I can help you see the significance of this. We know we are to seek His kingdom first, yet when we come to Him in prayer we start and stay with our kingdom. I believe God is waiting for us to ask for His **it**. Let me give you some examples of where the church effectively does this.

1.) VACATION BIBLE SCHOOL (VBS)

Every year VBS is the number one evangelistic tool for the evangelical world. God has used it to reach multitudes year after year. But have you ever thought of the amount of prayer that goes into VBS? For months the teachers, the students, the families are prayed for. The whole church is mobilized in prayer for VBS and God honors those prayers. The church at that time prays in one accord for VBS.

2.) REVIVALS

The most effective revivals are those that have truly been prayed for. Churches that utilize cottage prayer meetings, solemn assemblies, fasting, and unified focus prayer for revivals generally experience revival. I do a lot of revival meetings and I can tell where the church has been seeking the face of God for revival and the ones where they just added it to their prayer list.

3.) CRUSADES

If you have ever been a part of a crusade, you know what I am talking about. Teams will come in months prior to the crusade to train and mobilize intercessors. As the crusade approaches, the intensity of the intercession builds to a climax. As the crusade begins, people come expecting God to do BIG things. The level of anticipation has grown as the intercession has grown. Churches across the county, city or area have been united as one voice for one thing—revival.

4.) MISSION TRIP

Having served for several years as an international missionary and having led many mission teams, I know firsthand the power of the prayers that go into a mission endeavor. It doesn't matter if it is a youth group going across the county or a team of believers going across the world, where God's people are mobilized into a concert of focused and unified prayer God moves.

5.) INTENTIONAL PRAYING FOR THE LOST

In my travels, I have witnessed just about everything done to bring God's people to bear on the salvation of lost people. I have seen altars covered with names where God's people were given permanent markers and instructed to write the names of lost people on the wooden floor of the altar (and, yes, that pastor is still there). I have seen wooden crosses covered with pieces of paper of names of lost loved ones stuck to it. I have seen numerous boxes filled with the names of lost people. I have seen intercession thrusts for the lost that have revolved around names on cards. Rocks and crosses in pockets to remind people to pray for their lost friends. Regardless of the means, focused prayers for the lost seem to be something God honors.

Why does God answer these prayers? They are all about His revealed will for us. The calling prayers come from an awareness of what He desires for our lives. The Kingdom prayers we are simply praying what He told us to pray for. These issues reflect His **it**. Do your prayers reflect His **it**? If you are going to shepherd His people in prayer that is powerful and effective, then you will have to lead them to seek His **it**.

6

PETITIONING FOR IT

Doña Juanita was a little old lady in our church in San Ignacio, Belize. She had been sick for a few days and someone had recommended a home remedy. She took their advice but got some of it mixed up and nearly killed herself. She had taken some Kool-Aid, Bengay, other over-the-counter meds, mixed it all together, and drank it. You can imagine what the Bengay did to her. Her husband rushed to our home almost dragging us back to their little house. When we arrived, there were already several people from the church there. I remember thinking poor little Doña Juanita was not going to make it. She and her husband begged for us to pray. We gathered around her little bed, and we prayed with all the faith and fervor we could muster up. As we prayed, God began to work in her body. By the time we left that little home Doña Juanita was sitting up and doing incredibly well. God healed her little body, and He grew our faith.

Cholera is a terrible deadly disease. A person dies of dehydration from it in a matter of hours. It takes the lives of the young, the old, and the weak. Cholera came down the river and waters of Guatemala and Belize on two occasions while we lived there. Burying little bodies is not one of my favorite memories of serving in that part of the world. Early one morning, I was awakened by the cries of a very desperate Mayan friend. As I approached the gate, I could see his grief and his fear. As soon as I was close enough, he started to let me know his son had died in the night, and, most in his family were very sick as well. We climbed in to my vehicle, raced to the river, and ran down the bank to his little thatched roof shack. You could feel grief and death in the air. As I entered the room, there awaited his family all huddled around a little boy wrapped in newspapers lying on a bed of planks. They were all so sick. The wife held tightly to a little toddler that was so weak from cholera. I carried the dead child to my vehicle, and the family all climbed in. I rushed them to the hospital and waited. The doctor said all but the father and the eldest son had cholera. The child had to be buried immediately due to the disease. So the father, eldest son and I spent the rest of the afternoon building a wooden box and digging a grave. While we were lowering the little box into the grave, the father finally broke down and wept. He begged for me to pray for him and his family. He had not asked prior to this time, but I had been in constant prayer the whole time. As he stood in the grave of his son, I prayed with him. Sometimes it takes a lot for people to ask God to do something for them.

Petitioning is asking God to do something for you. (Intercession is when you ask God to do something for others.) Asking for something for ourselves makes God personal and intimate. When He responds to our petitions, He is saying something about His love for us and His value of us. His answers to our petitions become a part of our personal testimony and journey. It helps us grow in knowing His love, His power, the length of His reach and His heart. Each time He responds to our cries, our faith grows. Can you remember the last time He responded to your personal cry for help? Do you remember how that encouraged your faith? In Jeremiah 33:3 God urged Jeremiah to ask of Him. God promised to do great and mighty things, things Jeremiah knew not. Now think about that. God says to Jeremiah, "Ask!" But God promises to do what Jeremiah doesn't know to ask. Can you ask for what you don't know to ask? No. God is saying, "I am going to honor you, Jeremiah, by not doing what you ask, but by doing more than you can dream to ask." What kind of God do you have? One who only does what you ask or One who does what you don't know to ask? I am glad my God does more than I can ask, and that He does what I know not to ask. There are many reasons why God answers my personal prayers, but one of the "biggies" is so I will grow in knowing Him more. Every time He answers me I grow in my understanding of Him.

Some think it is wrong to ask for anything for themselves. Satan seems to enjoy convincing men that this is a truth, but it is a lie rooted in pride and self-righteousness. Petitions are encouraged by God and welcomed by Him. God invites us to ask for ourselves, and He warns us that we can even go without things He would like to give us if we do not ask. To ask for others requires very little humility, but to ask for self requires humbling oneself. To ask for self requires we admit there is something in our life we cannot do on our own. It is a cry for help and proud people do not ask for help. The parable of the Pharisee and Publican teaches us it is the man who humbles himself that receives. If you look at the prayers of these two men in Luke 18 you quickly see the Pharisee asks for nothing. Why? Because he didn't think he needed anything. The Publican, on the other hand, does not hesitate to ask. Why? Because he was very aware of his need and very aware of who he was and who God is. A wrong understanding of who self is will cause an individual not to ask for self. But a wrong understanding of who God is will also cause an individual not to ask for self. Some say things like, "Well, God has so much to do, and I don't want to bother Him with my stuff." This originates from a view that God is limited. This person makes God in his own image. This person sees God to be like man–limited; thus, he believes God can become too busy or have more important things to do than answer him. He tries to protect God, like God needs to be protected. God never has too much to do! God can never become overloaded or overworked! God is not limited in any way.

It is not unusual for some to pray and never pray for self. Many do not even think to ask themselves, "What is the one thing I long for God to do in my life?" I have found asking this question regularly allows me to take a spiritual inventory of my life. It allows me to seek to look at what is weak, what is lacking. When it comes to asking, we can focus on the situation at hand or we can focus on the Supplier—God. When you find yourself in a bad situation, the tendency is to stare at the walls of the pit and cry for deliverance or the removal of the crisis. But remember that God is perfecting us and making us complete in every situation causing us to ask for the necessary supplies that will carry us through the present situation so we are stronger and more complete afterwards and not just delivered from the crisis. Being delivered is not always what we need, but being made complete and lacking nothing is.

Asking for your **it** is a very humbling thing for most men. Most men just do not like to admit there is anything in their life they need help with or that they are weak. This is pride. God knows this and directs most of the directives to pray toward men. Men need a little more help to ask. They don't mind asking for someone else but not for themselves. This is what is so amazing about Paul. Paul is constantly asking others to pray for him and the most common prayer request of Paul is for boldness. Just a reminder in case you have forgotten—**You ask for what you know you don't have and know you need**. Paul was constantly asking them to pray for boldness because he lacked it and needed it. When we see Paul, we see him after his prayers have been answered. In other words, we see a bold Paul because he asked, and God gave. Note that Paul did not just ask the "Peters" of his world, he asked regular believers to pray for him. This is unusual for most men. Most men ask those they think are more spiritual than they are to pray for them. Paul did not ask those who he saw as greater than himself or who were more spiritual. He simply asked the CHURCH! Why? Paul knew that the power of prayer did not rest in the ones who were spiritual, but in God! Asking is an acknowledgement of need and weakness. God loves it when we acknowledge our need for Him and Him alone. God is not deceived by what is true humility. He looks for it in the closet of prayer and in the house of prayer.

When we served as missionaries in Belize, it was a normal part of our family's life for people to ask us, How can we pray for you? We never failed to seize the moment and to direct them how they could pray for us. But asking people to pray for us is very different than asking them to pray for you. And it is another whole different thing for you to tell people how to pray for you when they ask than it is to go to them and ask for them to pray for you. The challenge in James 5 is for the sick and the afflicted to ask others to pray for them. It is one thing for me to ask you to pray for someone sick and another thing completely for the sick to ask. Each year as my family shares our **its,** we are forced to ask one another to pray for us specifically. Each year I have to search my heart concerning what I should ask them to pray about for me. Do I ask something very general and superficial? Do I ask for something deep and life-transforming? Do I ask in a guarded manner or do I ask in a very transparent way? Do I hide what I really need God to do or do I truly confess my faults?

In recent days I have been truly overwhelmed by the tasks at hand. I feel so much like the *least of these*. I find myself wondering, "Who am I that you would give to me such a task." I have asked my wife to pray for me for strength and inspiration. I have asked others to pray that I will have wisdom. God is providing those things but as time goes on, I find the one thing I need most I have not asked for nor have I asked others to pray for: the hallowing of His name in me and in all I do. Hey, I just stopped and asked for it to be done! That is the incredible thing about God and prayer, I can ask anytime and anywhere! Now that is what I am talking about!

Will you humble yourself and ask for what you need? Will you make your **it** known to God? Will you humble yourself and ask others to pray for you? Do you dare ask your church to pray for you? Can you take that risk? Are they trustworthy enough to pray for you if you asked them or would they simply put your name on a prayer list and leave it at that? When was the last time you said, pray for me, not pray for them or pray for us?

7

INTERCEDING FOR IT

I could share countless examples of prayers of intercession. We generally are quicker to ask God to do something in the lives of those we love than we are to ask Him to do something in our own lives. I will only share a few. I am sure you have a list of your own that this section will call to your memory.

I was conducting a revival in lower Kentucky in the Land between the Lakes area. It was a good little church with a pastor that had been there for many years. He loved the people, and they loved him. It was during the second Sunday morning service when the events I am about to share with you took place. It was about halfway through the service that I first saw J. J was a very large and strong man dressed in black leather with decals all over his vest. His hair was long and his beard was full. He took a seat near the back and kept his eyes fixed on me the whole time. As the preaching came to an end, many people began to fill the altar. There was a lot of emotion in the room that morning, and God was answering the prayers of His children. The pastor was at the altar praying with someone when J made his way to me. He grabbed me, and I was swallowed up in his beard and his arms. He wept like a baby as he begged me to pray for him. I prayed and soon he was praying. J gave his life to the Lord that morning in my arms (actually I was in his arms). My wife told me later that when J grabbed me nearly every man in the church came and surrounded us. She said it was nearly impossible to see me or J at that time. When the Spirit had released J, she said it was like layers being peeled off an onion as the men began to return to their seats. As all the men backed away, and J released me, the pastor was finishing up with the man he had been praying with. The pastor had heard the cries of the men but did not know what was going on. When he saw J release me, the pastor was overcome with emotion. He lunged for J and the two of them hugged and cried together. The pastor told me later he had prayed for J for 15 years! He had gone by his home many times, but each time J would run him off. God heard the intercessions of a pastor for one lost sheep in his community and saved a son of the founder of the Hell Angels that morning—J.

It was another Sunday morning, and I was preaching in Springfield, Tennessee. The church was full and the altar was, too. As the pastor and I were ministering to the troubled souls at the altar, a piercing scream was heard ringing throughout the room. All eyes turned to see what was happening. I could just barely see the head of a man in his mid-40's walking up to the altar. In the middle of the pews was a woman being held tightly by her husband. She was screaming and crying with unbelievable release. The pastor knew the man coming down the aisle, and he ran to meet the man. The man crumpled in the pastor's hands. The man's cries for God to forgive him and to save him could be heard over the cries of the woman. Soon the woman, her husband and many others flooded to the man who, by this time, was on his knees before the altar. They all prayed and rejoiced together. I discovered later it was the man's mother that had let out the piercing cry. It was his family that had surrounded him. They had prayed for his salvation for years. He had spent the better of two decades in homosexuality and, on that morning, God saved him and delivered him. Now that is the power of persistent intercession!!

For those who believe God answers them, it is an easy thing to pray for those they love. In fact, praying for others is just the natural thing to do when you believe in the God who answers His children and you love someone who stands in need of a work of God. When you believe God answers you, there never seems to be a shortage of those for whom to pray. Living in a fallen world constantly drives us to God. Heart cries and mind cries are not the same. We know God desires to hear from our hearts and not from our lips. *This people draweth nigh unto me with their mouth, and honoureth me with their lips; but their heart is far from me.* (Matthew 15:8) Yet, we still have a tendency to be a people that draw near unto Him with our lips and honor Him with our mouths while our hearts remain far from Him. God wants our hearts and not just our prayers. Our **its** should come from our hearts. You won't have many of them at a time, mainly because He just hasn't made us to be passionate about a lot of things at once. But watch out when one thing or one person grabs our hearts.

This year my daughter and son-in-law's **it** was that God would save their son, Grant. We all eagerly embraced that **it** and in April, just four months into praying, God saved him. Our family has seen God answer our **its** so many times that we approach the throne of God with eager anticipation of what God is going to do. Where have you seen God answer your **it** as you have interceded on the behalf of others?

Two things we need to remember when interceding: we are never alone and we are never the first to do so. The great Intercessor, Jesus, always beats us to our knees. We are always coming alongside of Him. He is the one who has invited us to pray for one another, and it is His lead we follow. The Son and the Spirit are always at the side of our brothers and sisters before we can ever get there. They are in a state of intercession before the ones in need even know to do so. The Holy Spirit convicts us, burdens us, and calls us to join Him and our Lord in praying for our brother or sister in need. In intercession, we find ourselves in good company. I believe the strongest **its** I have had came from them and not from me. I simply found myself adding my voice to theirs. What a holy and sacred trust we have been given. To intercede for someone else is an expression of our faith and love. To intercede is a statement to the person that we are praying for that they are of great value to us. To intercede for them says we believe God will answer us for their good. When we are interceding for someone, we have entered into the holy of holies and take our position alongside the Son and the Spirit.

In Luke 8 we find Jairus coming and asking for Jesus to heal his daughter. Jairus' **it** was for the life of his daughter. In Matthew 17 we find a father coming to Jesus asking Him to heal his son. It is not uncommon for me to hear parents asking God to do something in the life of their children. Their child's need becomes their **it**. Several of my present **its** are for God to do a work in the life of my children and grandchildren. Many times my **it** has been for a lost loved one or for someone sick or hurting. These **its** become my **it** as God creates awareness of their need.

Those who have burdens for true revival and awakening often find themselves consumed with this **it**. Their love for the will of God and for their nation causes them to cry out with great heaviness and sorrow. They can't seem to escape this **it**. **It** goes with them everywhere they go and shapes all of their prayers. The cry for revival for them is not isolated to a few days or to a couple of worship services. They long for the eternal transformation of lives by God's hand and they can know no rest.

Some **its** are short-term prayer requests, while others seem to stay with us until the end of our lives. My wife and I have an **it** we have prayed since our marriage. There is rarely a week goes by that one of us fails to ask for **it**. That **it** is, "May our seed and our seed's seed be found faithful unto you until you come." We long for all of our children and for theirs to know the Lord as we know Him (even more so). This prayer has influenced all of their prayers. When our daughter suffered a miscarriage, I prayed this prayer constantly. When she suffered another miscarriage on the same day as the first a few years later, I prayed this prayer even more so. When my son and his family answered the call to preach the gospel and made the move to Canada, I prayed this prayer with a new found fervor. As my grandchildren grow older and the temptation and pressure of the world comes upon them, I pray this prayer even more. I don't know what the unfolding of this prayer will mean in the lives of my family, but I do know the end result I long for—their faithfulness until He comes. Some of our **its** are temporal and temporary while others are of heavenly importance with eternal significance. Some of our **its** are greater than any given situation and are not crisis or situational in nature.

Some **its** we initiate because we see or know something the person we are praying for is unaware of. Some will never call us to pray for them because they do not know their need. A few years ago I became extremely burdened for my eldest brother who was lost. That burden grew until one night I wept uncontrollably for him. My children were with me at the time and asked why we were praying and crying for my brother. Their question was, has something happened to him? I shared with them nothing had changed, but I believed God had burdened me to pray for him because he did not know to pray for himself. It was true then and is still so today. My brother does not know of his need and, thus, he does not pray. So I must intercede for him. I know something he does not know.

Other intercessions are initiated by others. Their call for us to pray creates the awareness we needed to put our faith and love into action. Someone receives a call that someone is in the hospital, the situation is critical, and immediately a call for prayer sounds throughout the church. Sometimes we are asked to pray for someone for their **it** only to find out as we pray God has a greater **it** in mind and He changes our hearts and our prayers change.

Though intercession can be a private thing, it is never impersonal. In fact, in most of the examples of intercession, it is a prayer of presence—physical, mental, emotional, and spiritual. The model for praying for the sick in James 5 is one of physical presence, how else can you anoint with oil? The pattern of Christ was one of intercession as Emmanuel, *God with us.* Rarely is He found healing without being physically present. Intercession does not require physical presence, but it does require presence and emotional intimacy with the person being prayed for. Intercession should be intimate and personal, more than private and distant.

For whom is God calling you to intercede? What is **it** He waits for you to pray in their life? Keep your eyes and ears open, He will be inviting you to intercede very soon. When He does, remember you won't be alone, the Son and the Spirit will be there before you will. Squeeze in between them and really listen to how they are interceding and make your prayers sound like their prayers.

8

CONFESSING IT

Psalm 66:18 states, *If I regard iniquity in my heart, the Lord will not hear me.* This is not a lost man that pens these words. This is a child of God, a believer, probably King David. This is a man God has filled with the Holy Spirit in order to write Scripture. This is all about what happens if a believer regards sin in his heart. This is about relationship, our relationship with the Father. This is about what you do when God says, That is sin, and it must go! Do you regard **it** or reject **it**? Do you cherish **it** or forsake **it**? As a believer, only when God reveals sin in your life do you have the choice to cherish **it** or confess **it**.

This person has heard from God. A decision must be made. Will they listen to Him? God has identified the **it** that needs to be confessed and forsaken. At that moment the person has a choice to heed or reject the voice of God. If this person refuses to listen and heed the voice of God, then he can expect God not to listen to him. God has revealed His **it** by convicting and rebuking him of his sin. This man has heard from God, and God has directed him to act accordingly. If he continues to cherish this sin in his heart, then he should not expect God to hear him. Why? Because this person is not hearing or listening to God. God loves him and cannot continue to walk with him as though nothing is wrong. This man refuses to listen to the voice of God concerning his sin; there is nothing else God has to say to him. This man needs to obey the voice of God if he intends to walk with God.

This is not about perfection; this is about righteousness. This is about what a believer is supposed to do when God reveals sin in his life. God expects repentance that produces confession and forsaking of sin. To continue to ask for our **it** when we are not listening to His voice is futile. If we will listen to His voice and obey His command, He will honor us by forgiving and restoring our fellowship with Him.

A few years ago I was doing a prayer conference in East Tennessee on the Prayers of Crying Out. The church had entitled the conference "Hear

Our Cry" and placed a banner with those words above the baptistry. I was four hours into the conference, and we had just returned from a break. I was sitting thinking about the next session while they were singing when I started to mentally read the banner over and over again in my mind. I noticed they had put a picture of Jesus praying at the beginning of the banner for decoration. They had also left two other banners up in the church all the time. The conference banner was placed in between the other banners. As I sat there running the title of the conference through my mind, I started to whisper what I was looking at. My attention went to the other two banners, and this is what I heard God saying to me. "I am King of Kings, Hear my cry for I am Lord of Lords!" The more I read it, the more I realized God was changing the course of the conference to suit His needs. I got up to teach and read the three banners as they stood on the wall. I then said, "Which is more important, for God to hear our voice or for us to hear His?" We all realized it is always more important for us to hear His voice before He hears ours. In fact, we have nothing to say to Him until we hear His voice. We are unable to ask for salvation if He does not draw us and call us to Himself. We cannot give Him thanks or praise if He does not speak to us of who He is and what He has done. We cannot pray according to His will if we have not heard from Him concerning His will. We cannot confess if we have not heard from Him concerning our sin. If we do not hear His voice, He will not hear our voice.

Scripture speaks of three things which are critical in all prayers of confession—confession of sin, confession of need, and confession of lordship. The confession of lordship is always primary. We confess sin because He, our Lord, has convicted us of our sins. He convicts us of sin so His lordship can be restored. We sin and continue to sin because we are rejecting His lordship in that area of our life. He will not tolerate us having other lords. He convicts of sin because sin is where we manifest the reality of our rejection of His lordship.

We confess need because sin always creates great need, a need that cannot be met without Him. We need forgiveness, mercy, help, strength, victory and restoration. We need a Savior. Jesus is not just the Savior, He is Lord. Lordship is the main issue of confession, and confession is never complete without it. That is why He cannot hear us, because we are living as though we are lord. It is foolish to think that if we reject His lordship over any sin in our lives, He still has to hear us. When we refuse to humble ourselves before Him as Lord, we should not expect Him to hear us. The greatest sin in this is not that we remain in the present sin, but we add to our sin by rejecting His lordship in every area of our lives. Refusing to submit to His lordship and cherishing sin is nothing but pure rebellion against Him as the King of Kings. Confessing **it** is a must if we are going to have a hearing with God. In other words, we must first hear Him if He is going to hear us.

In October 1904 Evan Roberts, a young man chosen by God to be an instrument of revival in the Welsh Awakening, had one message with four points—

1.) Confess all known sin
2.) Deal with and get rid of anything doubtful thing in your life
3.) Be ready to obey the Holy Spirit instantly
4.) Confess Christ publicly

Evan Roberts understood confession was an outflow of a repentant heart and repentance involved confession, forsaking and surrendering to the lordship of Jesus Christ.

Have you ever met a man who admitted he was a sinner but who had no intention of seeking deliverance from his sin? It is a common characteristic of mankind. To name your sin does not mean you want deliverance from your sin. I often hear people say, "We all have our sins." They say this not in a state of remorse or repentance, but in order to justify holding on and remaining in their sins. God does not want us to just acknowledge our sins, He wants us to turn from them to Him.

Have you ever met a man who admitted he needed deliverance from his sin and needed a savior, but refused to submit to Jesus as Lord? Of course you have. It is a common characteristic of mankind. To name your sin and to acknowledge your need for a savior does not mean you are ready to give your life to Jesus as Lord. Biblical confession requires all three confessions—sin, need, and lordship, but there is always a greater emphasis on the lordship. Remember—we sin because we are rejecting His lordship over our lives in that area. Man needs God and not just forgiveness. God is sovereign, the ultimate sovereign one, there is none other. God chooses to grant forgiveness to those who make him Lord.

What has He called iniquity in your life? What is **it**, the sin, which needs to be confessed? What is **it**, the need, which needs to be confessed? What is **it** that is not surrendered to His lordship? God is waiting on you to surrender to His lordship in all areas of your life. He waits on you to hear His voice and obey before He will hear you. What is **it** that needs to be confessed and forsaken in your life? Is He waiting on you? Do you have a reoccurring sin in your life? Is there an area of your life you have not yielded to His authority?

The people of God can find their prayers unanswered because of corporate sin as well. The following passages are worth looking up—Isaiah 1; 59:1-2; James 4:1-4. Why did their prayers go unanswered?

Are the prayers of your church hindered? Could it be the tolerance of sin among you causes all of your prayers to be hindered? What is the reoccurring sin among the people of God where you worship? Are you just ignoring **it** as though it will just fade away? Have you, as a people of God, confessed it? As a people of God have you acknowledged your need before Him and surrendered to His lordship? What is the **it** that causes your church to stumble? As a people of God have you ever asked God to break its hold on you? Is He waiting on you to confess and to forsake ungodliness among you or are you deciding to regard **it**? When a man or His people come face to face with the Holy, Holy, Holy God, we should only have one response, *I am a man of unclean lips and I live among an unclean people.* May you hallow His name by honoring His voice and turning from your sin.

9

GIVING THANKS FOR IT

It is a good thing to give thanks unto the LORD, and to sing praises unto thy name, O Most High: (Psalm 92:1)

O Praise the LORD, all ye nations: praise him, all ye people. For his merciful kindness is great toward us: and the truth of the LORD endureth for ever. Praise ye the LORD. (Psalm 117)

I thank my God upon every remembrance of you, (Philippians 1:3)

I have heard T. W. Hunt on many occasions and in one of his meetings he talked about how the prayers of thanks were responses to God's bounty. Bounty is an old word absent in our speech today, yet it communicates so well when one thinks about what we have received from God. The word speaks of abundance and, as a believer, we are all granted an abundant life. With all God has given us, giving Him thanks should be constant and spontaneous. In America, we have lived in a land of abundance and prosperity for so long that we think it is the norm and somehow it is a result of something we have done. We believe we are worthy of such blessings.

Often I find myself rehearsing the words of Abraham Lincoln, from March 30, 1863, wherein he, along with the Senate, issued a proclamation calling our nation to a day of national humiliation fasting and prayed these words—

> We have been the recipients of the choicest bounties of Heaven. We have been preserved, these many years, in peace and prosperity. We have grown in numbers, wealth, and power as no other nation has ever grown. But we have forgotten God. We have forgotten the gracious hand which preserved us in peace, and multiplied and enriched and strengthened us; and we have vainly imagined, in the deceitfulness of our hearts, that all these blessings were produced by some superior wisdom and virtue of our own. Intoxi-

cated with unbroken success, we have become too self-sufficient to fell the necessity of redeeming and preserving grace, too proud to pray to the God that made us! It behooves us, then, to humble ourselves before the offended Power, to confess our national sins, and to pray for clemency and forgiveness.

It is true we often fail to give thanks because we fail to connect the bounties of life with the Almighty God who gives all of life.

It is true the more we are aware of how God has blessed us, the more we will give Him thanks. When giving thanks, you can name specifically what it is you are thankful for. It is a rather elementary observation that seems to be forgotten today. Prayers of thanks in Scripture are a result of God's people expressing the marvelous grace and love of God as He has bestowed His bounty upon us. The prayers of thanks are directly connected to a received gift from God. In other words, when you give thanks there is no vagueness about what you are giving thanks for, you can name **it**.

Ten lepers are healed, but only one comes back to give thanks for his healing. Jesus takes the fish and the loaves and He gives thanks. We are directed to give thanks for all things, for all His **its**. In James we know we can count it joy for **it** all because He is at work in us perfecting and completing us so we lack nothing.

Those who have an **it** are quick to give God thanks when God begins to move and work in the midst of **it**. They are much quicker to give Him thanks than those who do not have an **it**. Those without an **it** often fail to give Him thanks for what He does because they simply don't see His hand at work. When a person has an **it**, there is a spirit of expectancy. They anticipate that God is going to respond to their cries and as soon as they start seeing His hand at work, they begin to give Him thanks for what He is doing. When He answers their **it**, they almost beat the angels in giving Him honor and glory. Having an **it** focuses our attention on what God is doing, and when He has our attention He loves to show us what He can do.

I believe one of the reasons God encourages us to bring our **its** to Him is so He will receive our praise and thanks. Last year my **it** was for my youngest brother to return unto the Lord. During that whole time of prayer, I was at full alert. I was in a constant watching and waiting mode. Every time I saw God doing something in my brother's life, I began to automatically give God thanks. When God brought my brother back to Him, I wept with gratitude, not just because God brought him back, but because God answered me. My faith grew, and with it, my praise grew.

Remember the story of the boy who swallowed the marble? When the boy vomited the marble out, we all exploded into uncontrollable praise and thanks for what God had done. When my wife was in a coma, I prayed so hard for God to heal her. Any progress I saw in her caused me to give Him thanks. When she was completely healed, I wept before Him in praise and thanks for what He had done. When we began to get threats on the lives of our children, we prayed for their protection. When a group of teens caught our son and tormented him, we prayed. When he led some of those same young boys to the Lord, we gave Him thanks. When someone we have prayed for to be saved is saved, we give Him thanks. Our daughter's **it** this year was for her eldest son to be saved. When he was saved, our daughter called us as soon as she could, and we all gave God thanks for answering our prayers. When we knew God was calling us to follow Him but lacked the understanding to know where He wanted us to go, we would pray for wisdom. When the Lord gave us direction, we gave Him thanks. When we saw Him leading and working in marvelous ways in the lives of our children after years of praying for Him to do so, we gave Him thanks. Thanks are always connected to a specific known blessing from God. When giving thanks you can name the **it** of your thanks.

Each year as our family shares our **its**, we often remember how God has answered our **its** from years before. Remembering these answered **its** increases our faith and puts us in a better position to pray. When your faith is high, you ask high, and when your faith is low, you ask low. Remembering what God has done in your life puts you in a better position to pray. Rehearsing the acts of God in your life is not about reminding God of what He has done, but is about reminding you of what He has done. In most of the solemn assemblies of Scripture, the prophet, priest, or king would rehearse the acts of God before the people. This rehearsing of God's acts of goodness reminded them who He was and who they were to Him. This rehearsing grew faith. This rehearsing gave birth to thanksgiving. In our culture we do not rehearse the acts of God enough. We run in and out of His presence. We often talk more about what we want or about what we have done when we pray than about what He has done. We often tune out as we read the prayers of Scripture where they spend considerable time re-telling the acts of God. We jump to what they ask for and fail to realize the asking may only take up a verse or two whereas the retelling takes up verse after verse. To us this kind of praying is a waste of time. We are often heard saying things like, is he preaching or praying. We think the person is trying to tell God something or to remind God. We fail to realize this is a natural response of a heart fully aware of what God has done and is simply saying thanks. We don't know how to say thanks like this. We fail to miss the acts of God, and so we simply are found saying thanks.

I challenge you to have an **it.** You will find yourself giving Him more praise than you ever did before. You will find your thanks will take on a whole new meaning. You will be like the woman who was overwhelmed with joy when she saw God answer her prayers for her adult son. He had been living a lifestyle of homosexuality for decades. When she saw him running to the front of the church to be saved, she could not control her joy and gratitude. She burst forth into shouts of thanks and ran down toward him faster than he had run to be saved. For minutes she was exploding with tears and shouts of praise. Her **it** had been answered. I believe the hardest I have cried has not been in times of grief but in times of great joy.

What is **it** you need to give Him thanks for? Who has He sent into your life you need to give Him thanks for? What is He doing in your life you need to give Him thanks for? What supplies has He provided you need to give Him thanks for? What is the **it** He desires praise and honor for? What is the **it** your family, your church, your nation should be giving Him thanks for? If you were to rehearse His great acts of mercy, longsuffering and grace He has granted to you, what would that sound like? I am certain it will con-tinue a stream of **its** He has answered in your life. Why don't you take the time to reflect and to rehearse the **its** He has answered in your life? When was the last time you counted your blessings? When was the last time you counted your **its** of thanks?

10

LAMENTING FOR IT

The prayers of laments are some of the most passionate of life. They are filled with deep emotional pain. The person hurts! They are filled with an incredible amount of grief. Something has been lost or is about to be lost. Of all the prayers, they are the most heart wrenching for the one who prays them as well as for those who stand near. Let me share a few examples.

A 17 year old boy lays weeping on his face lamenting over his sin. His body is heaving as his tears fall like a torrential rain. His cries are loud despite the hugs of his mother and a friend who try to muffle them. He laments over the loss of innocence … innocence given away to pornography. He longs for it to never have happened. Though it was only a passing thing, he cannot remove the images that now taint his young mind. He mourns for what he has lost. He wishes he had never taken that path. He laments over his **it**. His **it** is the sacrifice of holiness, innocence and purity for a fleeting moment of lust. He now has a new **it**—he longs for forgiveness and cleansing. His cries are like those of King David after coming face to face with the discipline of the Lord. And you? Do you find yourself mourning because of one stupid, careless act of unrighteousness? Or have you simply stopped hurting?

A strong man bows with his body in a heap over a mourner's bench, he can still see the divorce papers on his kitchen table, and he longs for what was. He laments over the loss of wife and sons due to some foolish lustful night. He cries repeatedly that he wishes he had never had wandered. He laments for his **it**—the loss of family, integrity, purity and respect. He has a new **it**, "O Lord, have mercy and restore!" Like the laments of Joel he cries for God to restore what the locusts have devoured. And you? Do you hurt over a loss?

A grandmother sits and weeps with her head in her hands as she laments over the decisions of her granddaughter. She yearns for the drugs and the downward spiral to come to an end. She has warned and she has preached. She has loved and forgiven countless times, but every time she looks upon her granddaughter's face she sees nothing but what the enemy has stolen, and she mourns. Her **it** is for years to be given back to one who is not old, for wisdom to return, and for respect to return to her grandchild. She has a new **it**—life for her granddaughter. True life, the kind only God can give is what she yearns for. She pleads not for herself but for someone that does not seem to know to plead. And you? Do you have someone that does not know to grieve or to plead?

A preacher lies at the altar mourning over the state of the church. He pleads for mercy immersed with deep sorrow over what has been done to the bride of Christ. He yearns for holiness, unity, love and power to return to the bride of Christ. He sees the faces of countless men and women who used to sit in the house of God but no longer want any part of it because they have been robbed by God's people. His **it** is for the church to be the church Jesus died for and meant for it to be. His grief offers him two choices to pray for—judgment or mercy. One would release his heart to a ravaging bitterness and anger. Which does he choose? He chooses to plead for a new day among God's people. He decides to make his **it** a cry for mercy and a cleansing. So he prays for revival, true revival. Some do not take this path, some give up. Some become cold and indifferent even in the midst of ministry. Some expect nothing, just more of the same. Some grow increasingly bitter and from their well-spring spew forth the same. Some just faint and fade away. But not this man, he still chooses to believe, and though he laments that which he sees, he cries to the One that is holy and the One with whom nothing is impossible. He dares believe revival is coming. His grief calls him to prayer, but his faith and love are reflected in what he asks. Hope lives in his heart and not despair. What about in your heart? What does the Master find? Oh, that God would grant us an army of preachers like this man and would rid us of those that have grown cold and hard.

A woman cries with incredible pain as she stares at her son in the casket and shakes her head screaming, "It did not have to be this way!" She laments not just for the loss of a son, but the son she once knew. She laments she did not recognize the signs sooner. She knows she could not have done much to stop the death spiral, but she grieves over what she did not do. Some laments are not warranted, and this dear lady holds herself responsible for what she is not. It is these I believe God laments over. If they could only grasp His heart, they would know He is not passing judgment on them. Her **it** is for a loss that is great and a pain that will not go away. Her sorrow over what is lost drives her to plead even harder for those she loves. She realizes the shortness of life and the importance of making the most of every moment now. Her **it** is for God to put a hedge of protection around those that remain. She does not want to go through this again. She pleas for God to redeem them. Her grief drives her to plead. Others would have stopped praying and gone to blaming, but not her. She cannot stop now, for now more than ever before she knows what is at stake. And you? Did you stop, give up or are you even more determined now to intercede?

There is a young man I know who is constantly in a state of grief. His grief is a God-given grief. He is like Nehemiah and many of the prophets of old; he mourns for his country. He yearns for revival of God's church and for an awakening among the lost. His **it** of lamentation has given birth to an **it** of intercession. He mourns for what could be in the church and for what could be in his nation. That mourning does not leave him in a state of despair but drives him to plead with hope for God to send His Spirit upon the land. I believe he is on good praying ground. His grief and hope have had a head-on collision, and he cries out! He cannot but express his **it**. Often this is true. When an individual is in a state of lamentation they also discover they also have a deep passionate intercession. Do you?

Today in my daily reading I read chapters 9 and 10 of Ezra and there found the lamentations of Ezra and the people of Israel. God's discipline has been strong upon His people, but in an act of unwarranted grace God has let some of the exiles return home. It is then Ezra finds the people of God had rejected God's counsel and had married the people of the land. This may not seem like much to us, since most of us probably are the people of the land, but it was an outright rejection of the revealed will of God for His people. By doing so, they also joined themselves to the gods of their spouses. Further wrath was brought upon them. Ezra trembles, pulls out his hair, tears his clothes and is filled with great heaviness. He falls before God confessing and lamenting over the sins of the people. His **it** is, "O my God, what have we done!" God lifts Ezra up, and a new day dawns for

Israel. It can for you, too.

Laments have a tendency to become the stories of our lives. For many their story becomes bigger than their faith. When that happens, they seem to pray less because they believe less. They begin to wonder if God answers them, and so they move into a prayer life devoid of power. God should always be bigger than our stories. You can let your story conqueror your faith or you can let your faith grow to become even stronger in the midst of your story. Anyone can have great faith in good days, but the test of faith is seen in the days of storms. Has your storm become greater than your faith? Perhaps your **it** is the loss of your faith. May you ask God to help you in your stories and storms of life, but may you never fail to ask Him to increase your faith in those times as well.

I pray your prayers of laments be few, but when they come may you know God is near. Our God receives our tears and our pains. He is the one who invites us to cast all of our cares (**its**) upon Him.

11

THE ITS OF THE EARLY CHURCH AND PAUL

I do not intend to list all the **its** of the early church or of Paul. I only want to stir your interest enough to listen to familiar passages and prayers with an ear for the consistent heart cries of God's people. I would hope you would ask a simple question—are my prayers and the prayers of my church anything like the prayers of the saints of old?

A common **it** prayer of the saints of old was for boldness. In Acts 4 the church is faced with imminent persecution. The threat is real and will soon become much than a threat. They have a choice—be silent and be disobedient to the calling of God or proclaim the gospel and be persecuted. They are a called people and they know this to be the will of God, they have an **it** command of God, the Great Commission. So what will they ask? They pray from their calling and not from their crisis. Yes, they are very aware of the crisis but deliverance is not what they seek. They seek the supplies they need in order to fulfill the will of God. In one accord they have just one prayer, one heart cry, one **it**. *And now, Lord, behold their threatenings: and grant unto thy servants, that with all boldness they may speak thy word, By stretching forth thine hand to heal; and that signs and wonders may be done by the name of thy holy child Jesus.* (Acts 4:29-30)

Do you know what happened next? God did as they asked. He granted them boldness. The persecution comes and increases with each passing day, but the church had what it needed to face it. A note of reminder—you ask for what you don't have and know you need. They asked for boldness because they were not bold. We see the early church bold because they asked, and He gave. Another note of reminder—fear is the opposite of boldness. They were truly afraid but they knew who could give them what they needed in the midst of their fear. I tell people all the time it is not about whether you are going to be afraid but which is going to be greater in your life—faith or fear. If your fear is greater than your faith, then your fear will conquer your faith. But if your faith is greater than your fear, then your faith will conquer your fear. Don't forget that God is constantly saying to people *fear not*. Each time He does so He is saying, Let your faith be stronger than your fear. Which is stronger in your life? Remember—in the midst of fear He is the one who cries *fear not,* but He is also the one who invites you to ask for the supplies He has to help you in your time of fear. The early church knew what supply to ask for—boldness. Do you?

In the last verse of Acts we hear these words, *...no man forbidding him.* (Acts 28:31) Some translations say, *no man could hinder him.* These words are a testimony of the ministry of Paul. If you are familiar with II Corinthians, chapters 6 and 11, then you know part of Paul's testimony was that many tried to hinder him from sharing the gospel. It appears almost every place Paul went he encountered direct opposition and hindrances, but he was undeterred. He had a calling, and he was compelled by an incredible love for Christ. He saw himself a debtor, a man ready to proclaim the gospel even to death. He was a man that could not be hindered.

In Acts 18:9 the Lord speaks to Paul in the night by a vision. The Lord says, ... *Be not afraid.* That is interesting isn't it? Remember God never says *fear not* to someone who is fearless. He always says it to someone who is afraid. For most of us we just can't imagine Paul being afraid of anything, but evidently Paul is afraid. When you look at the context of this passage he is not afraid of God, but is afraid of the situation he is in. The Paul we know is a man who is fearless. Why? If you look at Paul's primary prayer request, you can find a clue to this. Paul consistently is asking others to pray for him for boldness. Ephesians 6:19-20 records a prayer request of Paul. *And for me, that utterance may be given unto me, that I may open my mouth boldly, to make known the mystery of the gospel, For which I am an ambassador in bonds* (literally chains): *that therein I may speak boldly, as I ought to speak.* Remember—you ask for what you don't have but need. Paul lacked boldness, but we never see him that way because God supplied him with what he lacked and needed and what he asked for.

What do you lack? What is it that keeps you hindered? What is it God waits for you to ask for? What is the **it** you need in order to fulfill His calling for your life? Is it possible you do not have because you have not asked?

12

CONCLUSION

Around the beginning of the New Year I begin to seek for what my **it** ought to be for the next year. I want to know what **it** is He has for me to do. My **it** last year was Psalms 119:18 and 27, *Open thou mine eyes, that I may behold wondrous things out of thy law.* Open my mind that I may grasp the wondrous things of your Word. *Make me to understand the way of thy precepts: so shall I talk of thy wondrous works.* In times past my **it** has been the salvation of various family members. Sometimes it has been for wisdom for decisions I knew my family or I would be facing in the year to come. At times it has been for victory over satan and sins in my life or in the lives of those I love. Consistently, as a family, we have shared these very intimate **its** with one another and have covenanted to pray for each other's **it** throughout the year. God has shown Himself powerful in our lives. He has consistently changed our hearts to His when our **its** were not in tune with His. He has consistently revealed himself to be powerful and loving as He has moved in the direction of our **its**. The faith of my family has grown as we have in one accord prayed for one another. We share the heart cries of one another and the joy of seeing what God does as we have sought Him. Each year as we share our new **its**, our faith is always high. We pray from the workings of God in our lives, and it is with hope and faith we enter into covenant with one another for the new **its**.

I challenge you to search your heart. What is your **it**? Is your **it** the same as God's **it**? God wants your heart. He wants you to love Him with all of your heart. Your heart should belong to Him. He cares deeply for you, and He invites you to cast all of your cares upon Him. He waits for you to yearn for His **it**.

What is the one thing He is waiting for you to ask for? Is it wisdom? Is it discernment? Is it faith? Is it boldness? Is it unity? Is it forgiveness? Is it healing? Is it deliverance? Is it salvation? What is **it** He longs to hear you ask? What is **it** He waits for you to humble yourself and ask Him to do?